THE SECRETS OF MY LIFE

THE
SECRETS
OF
MY LIFE

Caitlyn Jenner
with Buzz Bissinger

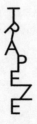

An Orion paperback

First published in Great Britain in 2017
by Trapeze
This paperback edition published in 2018
By Trapeze, an imprint of The Orion Group Ltd,
Carmelite House, 50 Victoria Embankment,
London EC4Y 0DZ

An Hachette UK company

1 3 5 7 9 10 8 6 4 2

A CIP catalogue record for this book is available
from the British Library.

ISBN (Paperback): 978 1 409 17396 0

Printed and bound by CPI Group (UK) Ltd, Croydon, CR0 4YY

The Orion Publishing Group's policy is to use papers that
are natural, renewable and recyclable products and
made from wood grown in sustainable forests. The logging
and manufacturing processes are expected to conform to
the environmental regulations of the country of origin.

www.orionbooks.co.uk

To the memory of my father, Bill, and my brother, Burt

Author's Note

This is a book primarily of recollections. I believe them to be true, and I have cross-checked them with various members of my family and friends and what has been written in the past.

But they are based to a large degree on my memory, and memory as we all know is selective. There is absolutely no attempt to color what I see as the truth for my own purposes: there is much I regret because of my own actions, just as there is much I celebrate. All I can do is write about them with sincerity and candor.

Transgender guidelines suggest that I no longer be referred to as Bruce in any circumstance.

Here are my guidelines:

I will refer to the name Bruce when I think it appropriate and the name Caitlyn when I think it appropriate. Bruce existed for sixty-five years, and Caitlyn is just going on her second birthday. That's the reality.

Contents

CONTENTS

Biology loves variation. Biology loves differences. Society hates it.

—MILTON DIAMOND

Prologue

I am at the Marriott Hotel in Orlando giving The Speech to the sales force at Merck.

Six in a row one after the other, the same words and the same message and the same title and the same feigned enthusiasm just like the hundreds of other times I have given it forward and backward across the country. It is the 1990s. But it could be the 1980s or the early 2000s. They have all merged together.

I know why people are here in the audience. They are coming to listen to the Bruce Jenner who won the decathlon at the 1976 Olympics in Montreal and became dubbed, as is the tradition, "the world's greatest athlete." They are coming to listen to the Bruce Jenner who saved the United States Olympic Team from terrible disappointment at the hands of the Soviet Union and East Germany during our nation's bicentennial year. The Bruce Jenner who literally overnight became an American hero. The Bruce Jenner who is the essence of virility and is the ultimate conquistador of women. The Bruce Jenner who gets anything he wants. The Bruce Jenner who looks at himself in the mirror and sees a stud among studs.

They don't know that when I look into the mirror I see something entirely different, a body that I fundamentally loathe: a beard that is always noticeable no matter how close the shave, a penis that is useless except for pissing in the woods, a chest that should have breasts, a face with a jawline too sharp and a forehead too high. They don't know that contrary to what they imagine, I have slept with roughly five women in my life, and I was married to three of them.

They only know what they see, which is the image I have carefully cultivated over those decades, which in turn is the image the media has bought into because it's the irresistible story they want to tell: the Olympian who rose out of nowhere and was the son of a tree surgeon and went to a tiny college in the middle of nowhere and married his college sweetheart and spent almost half his life to win the gold medal. In doing so I have also come to represent, perhaps more than any other athlete of modern times, the America of hard work and realizing your dreams in which we all believe. The America I believe in no matter how unbelievable I have become to myself.

They know what they want to hear, a life defined by those two days at the Olympic stadium in Montreal, July 29 and 30, 1976, when I broke the world record and ran around the oval of the track afterward waving a small American flag handed to me by an adoring fan.

THE SECRETS OF MY LIFE

I was happy then, incredibly happy, proud of my country and myself. And it took less than twenty-four hours for me to realize that the greatest diversion in my life, the Grand Diversion, the day-in-and-day-out training of the previous twelve years, was finished. Which raised the terrifying question any day and every day: what the hell am I going to do? What the hell am I going to do with my life? How much longer can I keep this up? How much longer can I hide and lie to those who still admire me and those I love?

I go to bed with frustration and shame. I wake up with frustration and shame.

They don't know that underneath the dark blue business suit I am wearing panties and a bra and pantyhose. They don't know that I am not Bruce Jenner but a woman I will come to call Caitlyn, who still has to be Bruce except for stolen moments here and there, twenty minutes or an hour or maybe two where I can feel what it is like to be my authentic self.

Imagine denying your core and soul. Then add to it the almost impossible expectations that people have for you because you are the personification of the American male athlete. You can't imagine it.

I am glad you can't. Because it is unimaginable. Except to me. Because I am living it. Or trying to live it. Because you don't really live. You just try to get by, pray that the conflict inside will, well, not go away completely, because you tried that already and it won't, but maybe take a breather, move to the background of your mind instead of the foreground.

Those in the audience don't know that despite my outgoing nature and a natural gift for small talk—because I do like people—I am always uncomfortable.

All they know is what they want to know. And all I know is to tell them what they want to know.

The speech I give to the Merck sales force is called "Finding the Champion Within." I have no need for notes. I know it by heart:

> I can recover from failure and go on with life and life will be good.
>
> We have to take fear and control it...
>
> You know when you're going down that road in life and that road comes to a fork and you gotta go one way or another...for some reason I always kept taking the right direction to go.

There was a time I believed those words, particularly in the aftermath of the Olympics, when I was preoccupied with the bounty of success. But now a certain word comes to mind:

Bullshit.

All bullshit.

Ladies and gentlemen, please give a warm welcome to Bruce Jenner!

I am acting here because that's how it has been almost

my entire life. I am playing Bruce because that's what the people listening to me want. That's what society wants. I get paid a lot of money for it. So I keep my mouth shut about who I am.

I finish up The Speech. I do the usual meet and greet afterward. I fake my way through by talking sports with the guys and making small talk with the women because I cannot relate what is in my heart. All I really want to do is get out of there and go up to my hotel room. The truth is I no longer give a rat's ass about The Speech. I do it so I can make a living, but I really do it so I can get out on the road. Because it is only on the road that I can feel any self-fulfillment; my wife, Kris, will not permit any of this behavior at home, just like my two wives, Chrystie and Linda, before her. She doesn't want to see it or deal with it, so we never talk about it. Why would she? She fell for Bruce Jenner, not some porcelain doll knockoff. They all did.

I wasn't totally honest with any of them. I was too ashamed. Too scared. But it was more than just that. Just like my ex-wives, I couldn't conceive of it either. Bruce Jenner?

Be serious.

Of all the people in the world, could anyone be more unlikely?

Bruce Jenner?

I lock the door to my suite at the Marriott and put out the DO NOT DISTURB sign. I order room service, a tuna sandwich and a Diet Coke, and tell the waiter to just leave the tray outside the door. I turn on the television to sports that interest me, car racing and golf. There are several mirrors in the suite, which I like. The bathroom also has a makeup mirror, which I also like.

I'm in business.

The ritual actually begins before I even get to the Marriott. It starts at Los Angeles International Airport, where I have taken every possible precaution I can think of to get through security without incident.

Nobody enjoys packing. But try packing for a man and a woman. I have a female friend who buys clothing for me since I am too scared to do it myself. I tell her what I need and she looks for it. But given that I am six feet two inches tall and can't try anything on in person, it's hit or oftentimes miss. Shoes are particularly tricky because of my big feet, good for the events in the decathlon but not so good when you are trying to dress up without detection. The selection is further limited because I am assiduously avoiding heels that are too high: the last thing I need is to be taller. So it actually makes packing easier since I don't have many options, either for this trip or the dozens of trips I have already taken.

I layer the outfits I am going to wear at the bottom, then I stuff a wig inside the sleeve of one of the garments and fold it over as extra precaution. I put my dark blue business suit on top along with assorted socks and shirts and underwear. This is before 9/11, so security isn't nearly as stringent as it is today. If I am stopped and my luggage is searched for some reason, I can always say that I packed for both wife and husband. I have an excuse ready for any situation. Always think on your feet. Deny, deny, deny. But I still want to avoid questions, and a woman's wig on the top layer is far more likely to cause snickers and speculation that Bruce Jenner is at a minimum an Olympian-sized kinkster.

I always bring a box of clear plastic wrap, which in my own homegrown method of feminization I cinch tightly around my waist to heighten my hips and buttocks. And let's not forget the little tube of Krazy Glue I use to do a makeshift facelift. After extensive trial and error and many different types of adhesives, I have learned that it adheres remarkably well, but it's a bitch to get off if you use too much, removing a tiny patch of skin and leaving a visible red blotch.

Fortunately I have gone to the bathroom before security to remove the breast prosthesis I am wearing. I actually forgot once, and the alarm went off as I went through the metal detector. As the officer positioned his wand on my upper chest, I was convinced the detector had picked up something on the bra. I braced myself for being marched to a private room to remove my shirt, and I am pretty sure saying the prosthesis was for my wife would not have worked. The fear was palpable, until it turned out that the wand had picked up a zipper on the rain jacket I was wearing. I was a lot more careful after that.

In this particular line of work it is always better safe than sorry.

I unpack and lay the clothing I will wear on the bed. Because I'm not one to experiment in a situation such as this, two items are almost always the same. One is a black dress with spaghetti straps at a length just above the knee, because if I know anything about myself, it's that the legs work. They have always been thin, much to the amazement of many, given my athletic success. I told them then that "my legs are made to go, not show." Now it's the opposite when I get the chance: my legs are there to show, not go. I can't say the same thing about my arms—definite no show—so the other item is a black jacket to hide them.

I stole the clothing from Kris's closet because it is quite sizeable and I do not think she will notice them missing. (By the time she discovered I had been "borrowing" them for several years, they had been stretched all to hell and she did not want them back anyway.)

It is my go-to outfit, cute but not too formal, complemented with black shoes because as we all know black makes you thinner. I have stolen makeup over the years not only from Kris but the rest of K-troop, Kourtney and Kim and Khloé and eventually Kendall and Kylie, because—trust me on this—there is more makeup per household user in our home than any in history. If you have watched *Keeping Up with the Kardashians* on the E! network, you probably know this.

Applying makeup is always the most intense, and I sometimes think I work harder on that than I did to win the decathlon. Although I have gotten better, it is still not a given as to how exactly I will look. In the past, I secretly bought how-to books since there was no one to help me. I keep the books, along with my meager collection of clothing, in a small closet with a lock and key in back of my own closet. Kris and I have negotiated this, since she is terrified, as I am, of the kids finding something.

It almost happened once with Kendall and Kylie. One suspected the other of stealing clothing—I don't remember who was the detective and who was the alleged perpetrator. I do remember that one of them secretly activated the security camera on their computer. With everyone out of the house I dressed up. I went into Kylie's room to check myself out because it had a full-length mirror. I thought nothing of it until later that night when I heard them running to their mother yelling, *Oh my God, what's on the computer screen?!*

They were mercifully too young to understand. It sounds funny now. It is funny. But not then. The embarrassment I felt was profound. I didn't want any of the kids to know. I didn't want to confuse them or scar them or hurt them. How could they possibly come to grips with this when not even I could? The episode was symptomatic of the tissue of lies I had built, never at peace with myself, total confusion.

Fortunately the episode was forgotten. But I learned a valuable lesson: whenever the woman inside you wants to check herself out in the mirror in your kid's bedroom, make sure the computer is turned off.

The eyes are the most important, because eyes of course are a window into the soul; you get the eyes right and everything else follows. They come out fine; I am definitely improving. But sometimes I get overconfident, and here I am, the world's greatest athlete, sitting there with my hands shaking trying to put false eyelashes on, which only results in black glue all over my eyelids.

I look at myself in the full-length mirror of the hotel room. I walk back and forth several times to make sure I am passable enough as a woman. I carry a purse—Kris's, of course, which is a little bit harder to "borrow" since she started keeping better track.

I leave the room. I usually take the stairs to the lobby to avoid getting stuck on the elevator with other guests. But I am on a high floor and don't want to exit looking a mess. So I use the elevator. I don't say a word because my voice, singsong and a little bit high-pitched, a combination of Midwest solid and Massachusetts twang, will give me away instantly after so many years in the public spotlight. I turn my back as if I am a disinterested, stuck-up broad, and I bend my knees a little bit to not look so tall.

I leave the elevator and walk around the lobby for twenty minutes, not a very good return on investment, since it took at least an hour to get dressed. It's exciting to me, and I sometimes wonder if that is the driving force, finding excitement in a life that no longer has any excitement unless you call playing golf by yourself exciting, and believe me it's not. Living with the Kardashian women and Kendall and Kylie is incredibly rewarding—don't get me wrong. They are dazzling, and in several years' time, *Keeping Up with the Kardashians* will draw millions of viewers worldwide. I come across in the reality show as a well-meaning but slightly doddering patriarch who has no life of his own and is subsumed by the women who surround him and only does what his wife tells him.

In other words: a totally true depiction.

I walk to the end of the Marriott lobby and then turn around and go back up to the hotel room. I never linger. I never stop. I never go to the restaurant. I look for remote crevices and corners. I try to avoid eye contact as much as possible although I am acutely aware that I am being checked out. As Bruce Jenner I have already been checked out thousands of times.

The reason for the looks is different now. I am not too worried about being recognized, because even if someone thinks they see Bruce Jenner in a dress (which they did), nobody is *still* going to believe they just saw Bruce Jenner in a dress because Bruce Jenner is the last person you would ever expect to be wearing a dress if you have the slightest memory of the Olympics. The reaction that concerns me is whether or not I am presentable. The length of the glance is the key determinant: a quick one means *no big deal, it's just another woman*. A longer one worries me, the implication being *what the hell is that?* Sometimes I think I look pretty darn good. Other times I feel like a thinner version of Big Bird, standing out for the world to see and snicker at after I pass. There are very few good things about getting old. Except that you shrink. So if I live to be one hundred, I will be five foot ten and maybe not feel so self-conscious.

I think about these things.

I remember once in another hotel how a man came up to me in the lobby. I was convinced this was it—busted. Instead he smiled and handed me a rose. I returned the smile and got away from him as quickly as I could. The last thing I wanted was a conversation. In the dozens of outings I have made to hotel lobbies over the years, I have *never* had a conversation with anyone. But I was flattered.

I leave the Marriott and get into my rental car and drive around for an hour or so. This is something I also would do, depending on mood and how much time I have. I see a strip mall and park the car on the outskirts of the lot, as far away as possible from any security lights. I walk around for a little bit, holding the car keys in my hand in case of an unexpected encounter that requires a quick dash back to the car. Thank God I am in sensible shoes. I do not stay out very long, but even the freedom of walking around in the farthest corner of a mall parking lot is still momentarily liberating. It *is* incredibly *exciting*—the pulse quickens, the heart rate rises, a combination of giddiness and confidence and daring the world and happiness, sublime happiness.

Going back so many years to the age of ten, I am still trying to figure out why. Am I truly gender dysphoric, clinically defined by the American Psychiatric Association as "a marked incongruence between one's experienced/expressed gender and assigned gender"? Am I maybe just a cross-dresser deriving some sexual high? Sometimes I wonder if dressing up like this is the equivalent of having sex with myself, male and female at the same time. I have no concrete answers.

Occasionally I venture out even beyond the parking lot. Like the time I was staying at the Opryland Hotel in Nashville. The Opry Mills mall is across the street. There was a multiplex cinema and I thought, *What the hell, why not go to the movies by yourself?*

I went over earlier in the day and had Bruce buy the ticket. That afternoon I gave the "Finding the Champion Within" speech. I went back to the hotel room and got fully dressed as the woman inside me. Then I walked to the multiplex and went right inside the darkened theater since I already had my ticket. I wanted popcorn—you have to eat popcorn when you are watching a movie, otherwise there is little point. But I was too scared to go to the concession stand. Fortunately the movie was good and I got into it, and for two hours everything else stopped.

I left the theater afterward and had to go to the bathroom. I doubt that for anyone else there it was a complex decision—you have to go, so you go. For me it was *Oh my God, now what am I going to do?* I had actually used the women's room before during previous outings. Like everything else I had a particular routine: I would wait outside to make sure no one else was entering. That way I could go in by myself and use the stall farthest away from the door. If somebody came in I would wait until she left. Then I would get the hell out of there.

The line for the women's room was lengthy that day. There was no way I was going to wait. So I scuttled back to the hotel as quickly as I could and made it up to my room.

I am still feeling good about myself when I get back. Nobody suspected anything. But I have an early flight tomorrow, which means Bruce will be back, rise and shine. Everything has to come off, unless I have a late departure. Then I sleep with the makeup on all night and it smears all over the pillow (sorry, housekeeping). Outwardly my life is good: terrific children, a strong marriage (at least before *Keeping Up with the Kardashians* takes off), steady work, a public that likes me. I continue to have a positive image.

It is not enough. It will never be enough. At this point in my life in the 1990s, in my forties, I honestly don't think I will ever get that peace in my soul. Concerns over family and the strictures of society are just too great.

I seriously think about putting a stipulation into my will that I be buried as was always my gender. Maybe that's the best and only answer to be the woman I always was, wearing what I always wanted for more than twenty minutes in a hotel lobby or going to a movie in the dark or driving around aimlessly.

That's the way I want to go to heaven. That's the way I want God to see me so I can finally ask him:

Did I blow it? Was there more I should have done?

I yearn for the answer here on Earth. But until I find it I do what I do best. I play Bruce.

—⁓—

Chapter One

A Stupid Boy

I have been divorced three times. I have given away enough furniture to outfit Ikea. I have lost too many homes to count. I have few pictures of my family growing up. When I separated from Kris in 2013 and moved into a rented house in Malibu, the entire home was furnished in a day with items from Restoration Hardware chosen by her and a crew of roughly fifty she assembled. I didn't even bother to take with me the gold medal I had won in the Olympics. Kris kept it in the vault for safekeeping.

I kept the accordion.

I wonder why it is the only possession of mine that has lasted through those three divorces and ten children and stepchildren, why I have lugged it around for close to sixty years since I last played it when I was eight or nine, why it is on an upper shelf in the garage of the home I now live in still in its original cumbersome case, collecting dust. It was only just recently I realized it was there, when I cleaned out the garage.

I think about many facets of my life, unequal parts wondrous and improbably absurdist. I worry about my relationship with my children and stepchildren, which I thought would make us closer now that I am Caitlyn but am so afraid has not. I think about whether to have the Final Surgery. I think about all the issues facing the transgender community and what I can do to help, because that has become a sacred commitment in my life. I still fear loneliness, just as I also know I am happier and more fulfilled than I ever have been.

The accordion is just an instrument taking up space, a relic of the long-ago past. But I believe that everything happens for a reason, so there must be a reason it is still with me. Sometimes I think if I can solve the riddle of its continued existence I can solve the riddle of my life: world record–setting Olympic gold medalist with no interest in ever truly competing in anything else ever again after I won, a fraud when it came to being my authentic self, public figure and private shadow, good father to my stepchildren but at one point abandoning my own children from my first two marriages, assertive yet deathly afraid of confrontation, a lover of people yet lonely, open yet absent of empathy, outwardly comfortable in my own skin yet inwardly desperately uncomfortable in it, wanting to be liked yet never quite sure I was liked because there were so many moments when I did not like myself.

I have felt different intensities of these feelings at different times. Some days were better than others. There were some days, even some blessedly long stretches, where

I didn't examine my soul at all or at least thought it was a phase that would pass or that maybe it could be cured—two aspirin and a glass of water and a clove of garlic around the neck and a rabbit's foot under the pillow.

For a long time I did not understand what was happening. There was no context or point of reference. The term *gender dysphoria*, increasingly and mercifully a growing part of the vernacular today, had as much application in the world in which I grew up as Facebook or Twitter or Instagram. Its first usage was not until 1974.

America in 1949.

It was four years after the dropping of the atomic bomb on Hiroshima, and Harry Truman was still president. The Volkswagen Beetle was introduced to America, Los Angeles recorded its largest snowfall ever, Rodgers and Hammerstein's *South Pacific* opened on Broadway with Mary Martin, and Howard Unruh became the country's first single-episode mass murderer when he gunned down thirteen neighbors in Camden, New Jersey, with a souvenir Luger.

Bruce Springsteen and Billy Joel were born that year. So were Meryl Streep and Sissy Spacek.

Then there was me, on October 28, 1949, the same day an Air France jet crashed into the Azores and killed all on board. But also the sixty-third birthday of the Statue of Liberty.

Typical of the conflict of my life.

My coming of age was the 1950s, the American age of the automobile and the creation of the interstate system under Eisenhower and McCarthyism and paranoia over communism, the age of *Gunsmoke* and *Perry Mason* and *Bonanza* and *Leave It to Beaver* and other shows in which virtually every major actor was a white male. In politics there were no African Americans in the US Senate and only one woman, Margaret Chase Smith of Maine, who had been elected.

I didn't know a single gay person growing up, or perhaps more accurately, I did not know a single person who would openly identify as gay because of the atmosphere that existed then. It is better today, but that same atmosphere still exists in too many places when it comes to being different from the status quo, which for me represents nothing except the arbitrary judgment of ignorant and hateful others.

Roughly a year after I was born, the US Senate Investigations Subcommittee of the Committee on Expenditures was directed to make an investigation into the employment by the government of what was termed as "homosexuals and other sex perverts." Among their conclusions and findings, which still bear repeating, was:

> The authorities agree that most sex deviates respond to psychiatric treatment and can be cured if they have a genuine desire to be cured. However, many

overt homosexuals have no real desire to abandon their way of life and in such cases cures are difficult, if not impossible...

These perverts will frequently attempt to entice normal individuals to engage in perverted practices...

The lack of emotional stability which is found in most sex perverts and the weakness of their moral fiber, makes them susceptible to the blandishments of the foreign espionage agent. It is the experience of intelligence experts that perverts are vulnerable to interrogation by a skilled questioner and they seldom refuse to talk about themselves.

To put it too mildly, it was hardly an age of enlightenment in the America in which I grew up. I wonder to what degree this environment influenced my conservatism, because I am sure it did. But it was also an age of increased bounty and consumerism—if you were white. Suburbs were rising, tens of thousands of affordable homes were being built, a middle class was burgeoning and booming. America was a safe and good place—if you were white—and I felt safe in that womb with my parents and my siblings as I grew up in Westchester County in New York and eastern Connecticut.

My father, William (Bill) Jenner, with a sense of humor as subtle and sly as his Boston accent was not, was emblematic of the Greatest Generation. He met my mother, Esther, at a roller skating rink in White Plains, New York, in the spring of 1942 after she had moved east from the Midwest. He was an excellent skater and was naturally skilled in many athletic activities. He had the ability to instantly master whatever he tried, a trait I was lucky enough to inherit. My mom was a wobbler on skates and slightly nervous as a result. She remembers it with her typical razor-edge bluntness:

Could I have this next skate?

Well, it's your funeral.

Esther was from Ohio and had spent a good portion of her youth on a seventy-three-acre farm at the top of a sloping hill near Shadyside, overlooking the Ohio River. Her father, a portrait photographer by trade, was a man of remarkable determination and focus in areas that intrigued him, essential qualities I inherited that served me in training for the decathlon. He built the house they lived in, sturdy and modest. In his spare time he was an amateur geologist, astronomer, and maker of telescopes. He loved to tinker and mechanically experiment. Just like me.

Bill had been born in the city of St. John's in Newfoundland and Labrador, Canada, moved with his family to Somerville, Massachusetts, and then Westborough. When he was young a terrible hurricane swept New England, downing thousands of trees. The logs were stored in lakes, and Bill's father ran a portable lumber mill, moving from lake to lake. Bill worked there for a year after high school and then moved to Tarrytown in Westchester County, New York, in the late 1930s.

Esther found Bill maddeningly handsome, and it sounds as if Bill did, too (clearly, vanity runs in the family). He was working for his brother's tree service and had a happy-go-lucky personality that Esther found infectious. They quickly fell in love, as many couples did back then, perhaps because they knew time was running out.

They got married in September 1942, when Esther was sixteen. America had declared war on both Germany and Japan, and Bill, like millions of young men his age, was desperate to fight. Because he was still a Canadian citizen, laws prevented him from enlisting in the US armed services. He could make himself eligible for the draft, but the minimum age then was twenty, and Bill was nineteen. On what seemed like a daily basis he went to his local army recruiter in New York to sign up for the draft. The recruiter finally could not take it anymore.

Have you got your birth certificate?

Bill produced his birth certificate.

Let me see it.

Yes sir.

The recruiter changed the date of his birth in pencil to make him twenty years old.

You'll hear in a couple of weeks. Now don't bother me anymore.

Three months into the marriage, Bill went off to the

army and Esther did not see him for three years. She wrote to him every day, even though she quickly ran out of interesting things to say. She worried about my dad, and there was ample cause for worry. He did not just want to be a member of the army. He signed up to be an Army Ranger, one of those often brought into the most intense and difficult combat situations. He trained as a member of the Fifth Ranger Battalion at Camp Forrest in Tennessee, then was assigned to Fort Pierce in Florida, where he got his first taste of what was in store when he was put out into the Atlantic by ship and then returned to shore in rubber amphibious boats with forty-pound packs. Bill was adept in the water, but some of his fellow soldiers didn't even have any idea how to swim. Nor were they asked if they could swim.

He was sent overseas to a base in Scotland for further amphibious and combat training. He was assigned to the headquarters division of the Fifth Ranger Battalion, in charge of eight soldiers whose job it was to keep lines of radio communication open between headquarters and units in the field.

He knew he was going to war.

Bill and his fellow soldiers received word of the objective three days prior, to be in the first wave that would attack the beaches of Normandy in what became known as D-Day. He and other soldiers were taken by ship across the English Channel. They started loading the amphibious boats at six a.m. on June 6, 1944. They were ten miles out and everybody was laughing at first, giddy for combat after two years of difficult training. The water was very rough. They had each been equipped with brown paper bags in case of seasickness.

My father was the toughest man I ever met. Nothing got to him. After the Olympics I bought a Pitts aerobatic biplane because of my love of flying and my penchant for pushing the limits. It was a two-seater with the passenger seat in the front. I was tested many times by friends who thought they were tough—*give me your best shot*—and they of course were the very first to get sick and plead for ejection. The only person who begged for more was my father. I tried everything—loops, double loops, spins, going as high as I could as fast as I could and then stalling and plummeting down before regaining control. I gave him all I got and he still wanted more.

Except during D-Day.

He did not get sick on the amphibious boat. But other soldiers did, violently so, those brown paper bags of little use. As they got closer to shore they could see shells exploding on the beach. Bullets whizzed by them. Everybody was quiet then. The giddiness of going into combat gave way to the reality of death and fire and blood and fear. Bill hit Omaha Beach into a swirl of chaos, the briefing they received useless. Running communications lines was hopeless, and placed him in the thick of combat with a submachine gun he became proficient with during training. The soldier in front of him was brushed by an .88-millimeter artillery shell, enough to split his body open. Bill hesitated for a second. He wanted to do something. But regardless of what all the umpteen films and books say, the ultimate objective of every soldier who landed was self-preservation. So he kept on running to the seawall and crouched down with his entire body shaking. He looked behind him. An amphibious boat carrying flamethrowers was hit, and the boat exploded in a ball of fire. He saw men jumping overboard in flames and had to turn away. He wrapped the spurting hand of a fellow soldier who had lost several fingers. He watched as the officer in charge of communications went berserk from shell shock and tried to run away and had to be held down. He stayed in one spot for ten minutes, then, convinced the spot had worn out as a sanctuary from death, moved to another one. He painstakingly worked his way up the beach, which was littered with the bodies of American boys. Later, as he and members of his unit made it off the beach into a small French village, he would have to participate in the killing of two young French women who were married to German officers and acting as snipers.

My dad spoke little to the family about the experience of D-Day as we were growing up except for the acknowledgment that what saves a soldier in horrible combat is luck.

It wasn't my day to die.

But every now and then a story came out.

I remember him describing the final minute before the amphibious boat landed. The English coxswain manning the boat stopped and wanted the men to jump into neck-deep water. Some fellow soldiers had already drowned because of the combination of current and waves and carrying one hundred pounds of gear. He refused to guide the boat any closer until an American officer on board put a gun to his head and said he would blow his brains out if he didn't get closer to shore.

My father said that did the trick.

The other story wasn't a story. It was a small and rectangular black and white photograph he took after his Ranger company had been sent to assist in the liberation and dismantling of the Buchenwald concentration camp in April 1945. It was the image of a railroad car flatbed piled five deep with the emaciated and naked bodies of victims like stacks of cordwood.

My father showed me the picture as a young boy. I did not understand why. It was completely uncharacteristic of him and far too extreme for any child of nine or ten to process. But it ultimately helped me to understand him, how his periods of silence were caused by things he had seen as a young man that he would always see for the rest of his life. It made him emotionally detached, a trait I would have in my own life.

Some people mention the word *bravery* in my transition from Bruce to Caitlyn in the spring of 2015 at the age of sixty-five. It is flattering. I certainly don't mind hearing it, and I appreciate the sentiment. But when compared to what my father and so many others went through, there is no bravery in becoming your authentic self. For me it was a form of cowardice to wait so long.

My father was a kind soul, even after all he had experienced during the war. He harbored no bitterness about anything or anyone—I am the same way in never harboring a grudge. I often wonder what he would have thought were he alive today. He loved my success in sports as I was growing up. His pride was indescribable when I won the Olympics. He reveled in my becoming an American hero. I often imagine the conversation we might have had. The reaction. The words he might say or not say. The look on his face. The one thing I never wanted to do was disappoint my dad. I always wanted him to be proud of me. He would not have understood my transition in a million years. He would not have been able to process it. Nobody of his generation would have understood it just as many millions today cannot grasp that transitioning from a man to a woman or a woman to a man has nothing to do with your sexual preference and everything to do with the gender that is embedded within you from birth regardless of your physical characteristics.

I know there would have been initial shock. But I believe that once he got over it and started to see the good I could do in a very marginalized community, he would have been as proud of Caitlyn as he was of Bruce. I know he would have wanted me to be happy. And maybe it would have made him happy to know that the turmoil in my life was finally over.

But it would have taken him a long time to get to any kind of acceptance. My mom, who knew him better than anyone, wonders if he would have ever come around on the idea at all no matter how he acted outwardly.

You have that image of your son, and that's the image you have, and then it's Caitlyn? Who is that? What is that?

I still would have wanted to tell him.

I never got the chance.

My dad went back to the tree business after the war, ultimately starting his own company and servicing some of the great estates of Westchester County and Connecticut. He was frantic to be a good family man, and he was. We did everything together as a family growing up. My parents dedicated every weekend to their children, my older sister Pam, then me, then Burt, and ultimately Lisa.

Our lives were pleasantly predictable, a two-week vacation every summer camping in the Adirondacks, a trip to the farm in Ohio where my mother grew up. I went to New York City exactly once before I left for college, even though it was less than an hour away by train, and that was only because of a school trip. I didn't meet a single African American until I was in junior high school. The outside world was largely viewed through *Look* and *Life* magazines. The idea that several years later I would travel the world over as an acclaimed athlete was nonexistent. The idea that there is a woman inside me was beyond nonexistent.

As I grew up I exhibited no outward signs of "femininity." I know that was puzzling to my mother and sister Pam after I told them I was transitioning. How could they live under the same roof with me during my childhood and adolescence and not see a single thing to suggest anything about me that was different besides perhaps an aloofness and discomfort with affection? Because there wasn't anything. I never felt feminine, but I did identify as female. What is femininity anyway? It is entirely what anybody wants it to be. Because I continue to love car racing and motocross and motorcycling, does that somehow make me less feminine? It is only our tired and backward definitions of male and female characteristics that may make it seem so.

When I was growing up, I hated having my hair cut. I hated going clothes shopping. Looking back, I wonder if these issues were an early sign of my gender dysphoria.

Or maybe I just hated having my hair cut and going shopping. There are some things in life you just hate because you hate them.

What I do know is the overwhelming insecurity I felt as a child was because of the difficulty I had reading aloud in school and the constant fear of being ridiculed. I always felt self-conscious, as if I didn't quite fit in, a social awkwardness that, while a thousand times better today, is still within me. I crave friends, which sometimes makes me do desperate things.

My father's pride and joy was his Army Ranger uniform. It hung in the closet, a row of medals across the breast of the jacket, including the Bronze Star. One day Pam, a year and a half older and about seven at the time, clamored for him to wear it. He went to the closet and took the uniform out, only to discover that the medals were missing. I hung tough under interrogation. It took me a long time to crack before I confessed that I had taken the medals and given them to someone whose friendship I yearned for in return for some ducks I could raise in the backyard. Tragically, the medals could never be located.

The ducks didn't last long, either.

Adding to my insecurities were the inevitable comparisons that were made to Pam. I idolized her. She was poised while I was not. She easily made friends while I did not. She easily blended into a crowd while I did not. She studied five hours a day to make straight As, while I studied five minutes a day to scrape by with Cs just so I could remain academically eligible for sports.

There was something distant about me. I was there but somehow not there, afraid of real emotion. I skimmed the surface because that was the only level I was willing to reveal because of what lay underneath, a sensation and desire pleasing and perplexing and puzzling. I was terribly at odds with myself, consumed by failure because of dyslexia and massive reading difficulties, and my poor self-image was only reinforced when I flunked second grade and had to repeat it. My mom went to school conferences frequently to figure out what was wrong. But no one was interested in trying to diagnose the problem, much less render a diagnosis of dyslexia, which in my educational setting was unheard of back then (a lot of things in my life were unheard of back then). It wasn't until junior high that a school counselor mentioned the word, then after ten minutes sent me back to class. Which left me with two enormous areas of my life that were undiagnosed growing up: dyslexia and the issue of my gender.

Teachers simply thought I was stupid. Or lazy. I did my best to be the teacher's pet, the goody-goody with or without an apple, so they liked me but still thought I was stupid and lazy. I dreaded going to school because of the fear that I would be called on to read and everyone would laugh at me.

There was also something else.

I was about ten.

The curiosity would not go away.

The object of it was in our second-floor apartment in Sleepy Hollow Gardens, a sprawling complex of sturdy and simple red brick at the south end of Tarrytown by the foot of the Tappan Zee Bridge, built in the postwar boom.

My mother's bedroom closet...

I was too young to even remotely figure out why I was so fascinated by its contents. While I know now that my issues went to the core of my gender identity, I sometimes wondered if I was somehow trying to emulate Pam. Because I idolized her, maybe that also led to envy and wanting to be like her. I was clearly grasping for explanations. All I know for sure is that I was powerfully drawn into that closet and the feeling didn't go away.

I was smart about this. I waited until I knew my parents and sister would be out of the house for an extended period of time. I slid the white particleboard doors open. I walked into my mother's closet. It was small because the apartment was small, just two bedrooms with a table in the kitchen where we ate most of our meals. My sister and I shared one of the bedrooms with a divider down the middle.

My mother's closet...

It seemed enormous although it was not. I looked at the dresses and the skirts and the shoes. I brushed my hand over them so I could feel the cloth and cotton. I glanced around to make sure I was alone. I heard nothing. I picked out a dress. I used a piece of paper to mark its exact position so I could put it back in the same place. I went to a drawer to get a scarf. I watched the way it was folded so I could fold it exactly the same way when I was finished.

There were no wigs around and my hair was cut fifties style, a patch of lawn down to a quarter inch. So I took the scarf and wrapped it around my head and tied it under my chin to make it look like a wig. My mother's shoes were too big, so I used my sister's. I probably stretched them out a little, but I was not too worried: not even Pam, as smart and savvy as she was, would ever suspect. I used a spot of my mother's lipstick. If she were to discover something amiss and I somehow got drawn into it, I had a plan for this as well:

Pam stole it.

It was the first of a thousand times I would have a ready-made excuse in case I got caught.

I looked in the mirror. Even then I felt the sense of freedom that I would experience thirty or forty years later in hotel rooms and lobbies. Something was right about this. But I couldn't tell anybody, so there was also more loneliness and isolation than I already felt. Even at the age of ten my life had become a sealed box, and over time, the sides would become even higher and ultimately impossible to scale.

Staying inside was not enough. I had to do more.

I left the apartment, checking for signs of human life. It was dark, because there was no way I would do this in daylight. I stayed within the confines of the complex, walking around the block once, up a hill and back down, then ran back to the apartment. The opportunities were rare, once every six weeks or so. I never saw anyone else when I went outside, except for this one time I walked down the hill and a car crept along behind me. I had my little dress on and my little scarf and I could feel the headlights. But then it went by me.

I just got away with it.

I don't know why.

The only point of reference I have is Christine

Jorgensen, the former army soldier who went to Denmark to have surgery and came back a woman. Outed by the *New York Daily News* in 1952, she fascinated the entire world. It was the prurience that intrigued the public as well as the medical advancement, a man becoming a woman, as if this were the next iteration of Frankenstein's monster, aberrant, abnormal, weird, wacky, secretly titillating to many who would never admit it.

I glean what I can about Jorgensen. But I am too young to make any direct link to what I am feeling. I only know it feels so right. I only know it feels so wrong. I have no life outside school, and school too often is something of a disaster because of my dyslexia. My self-consciousness is like a second skin. Now add wearing a dress and scarf belonging to my mother. I haven't even made it to *eleven* yet.

Cue the accordion.

With the exception of schoolwork, which I pretty much suck at except for math and mechanical drawing later on in high school, the accordion is the first thing I ever really try to do. I have two friends who have formed a little band together. One plays the guitar and the other the accordion. I cannot think of anything cooler than being in a band. But being uncool, I have no idea what cool really is. I love all the buttons on the accordion and the way you have to let it breathe in and out like a pumping heart. The guitar with those six lonely strings seems boring to me. So I go with the accordion, although in hindsight I now realize it would have been cool only if you lived in Sicily.

I tell my parents I want to play the accordion. I don't think this activity is quite what they have in mind as a hobby for me. But they are happy I want to engage in *something*, worried that I have already become a lost soul. An accordion is expensive.

So they go to my sister Pam:

Our parents came to me privately. Here I am, ten years old, and they said, "Bruce isn't doing well in school. He has this interest in playing the accordion and we want to encourage that because he needs to be successful in something." I could see this coming. Christmas is right around the corner. And they said, "You know, things are tight financially so we're wondering if you would not totally give up your Christmas but no big present for you this year because we need to spend several hundred dollars on this accordion." I was firstborn. I never did anything wrong. But inside I'm saying "hell, no." But what I said to them is, "okay." To this day I hate the sound of the accordion. To me it's like fingernails on the blackboard. And I had to listen to him practice.

It is painful at first, every sound like somebody wheezing to death. I have a fine teacher. I keep at it. I give a mean concert recital in my Cub Scout uniform. It is a pivotal moment, a glimpse that I can achieve something if I put my mind to it, actually be good at something. But rock and roll is beginning to take hold in the late fifties and early sixties, Elvis and Jerry Lee Lewis and Chuck Berry and of course the Beatles. None of them would be caught dead with the accordion. Here I am, playing oom-pah music, with a possible career on the polka party circuit. It gets to the point where I am afraid to tell anyone I play the accordion for fear it will just become another source of ridicule. So I quit.

As I said, there is a reason for everything in life. The hand of God takes you in directions you never consider, even when it involves the accordion. Looking back, I am happy I played it instead of the guitar. Had I chosen the guitar because of its cool factor, my guess is that I would have tried to get as good as I possibly could and would have become consumed with it at least through high school. I would have made it my calling card.

By giving up the accordion and concluding that a life in music was not for me, I was forced to find another outlet.

The one that saved my life.

June 13, 2015

"I was living in la-la land"

I am walking up to the front door of a home in Vista, California.

I am meeting with a mother and father whose teenage transgender son killed himself because of harassment and bullying on social media and in school, combined with severe depression.

I am trying to imagine the torment the teenager was in, but I cannot. He was fourteen years old. *Fourteen.* I am trying to imagine the pain of the parents and his sister, but I cannot.

I was admittedly living in la-la land the first few months after transition. I was in such euphoria becoming Caitlyn that the massive problems facing our community really did not register. I began to read studies. But statistics only show. They do not tell.

It is only when you look into the eyes of a mother whose transgender son committed suicide, listen to her ask what she could have done differently when there was nothing she could have done, that you begin to under-stand how becoming a trans person affects not just the individual but the entire family. The age of the person transitioning doesn't matter, because tragedy can happen at any age. What does matter is that for all the raising of public consciousness, there is still a marathon to be run, and I don't think it will be finished in my lifetime.

I need to listen to those who have been so terribly impacted. I need to say I am sorry, although the word has such little meaning. I need to shed tears of my own. It renews my commitment to change.

Which is what brings me to the front door of the home in Vista. I am greeted by Katharine and Carl Prescott. It was their son Kyler who took his own life in the bathroom of the family's home on May 18, 2015. According to his mom, it wasn't just depression and repeated cyberbullying that made life such hell for him; it was also adults who refused to accept Kyler or address Kyler by the correct pronoun even though he had legally changed his name and his gender marker.

I worry about transgender teens the most, although I am buoyed by the number of programs for gender-variant, gender-nonconforming, and transgender children and youth that I have made a point of seeing all over the country. But still I worry.

Statistics are useful: in a recent study 51 percent of transgender youth reported thinking about suicide, and 30 percent said they had attempted it. There has historically been a lack of acceptance of the LGBTQ community, and this has only been amplified by cyberbullying. Today it's even more awful than a group of kids in the school hallway gossiping about someone, because hurtful and malicious words posted online by cowards who hide behind the Internet never go away. By way of example, all you have to do is go on my Instagram account and see the comments to understand the level of vicious hate that is out there. When I write something positive about the trans community, I am met with comments beyond comprehension by transphobics, homophobics, and racists.

Kyler had tremendous courage. But courage is not enough. There has to be tolerance initiated by adults. The instant there is any cyberbullying on a social networking site, it is incumbent upon the powers that be to not only immediately remove the posts but also ban the users. This is not an issue of free speech. This is an issue of freedom of choice and self-expression and potentially preventing suicide.

"There is nothing more painful than losing your child. Nothing," said Katharine Prescott in an interview with the *New York Daily News*. "Kyler was the sweetest, gentlest human being. He wouldn't hurt a fly. The only thing on Earth he would hurt is himself. And if I can even help one family, one other transgender kid like Kyler, I will do it, because this has to stop."

Katharine Prescott shows me pictures of Kyler. She tells me of his love playing the piano. She lets me read a poem

Kyler wrote about transitioning. She talks with passion and beauty, something you can only feel when you are on the front lines. "I feel like I did everything possible to embrace his gender identity...but my child committed suicide anyway, and I've struggled with the unfairness of that."

I join the family and Kyler's friends at a memorial service at a nearby beach, where balloons are released in his memory. The kids ask me questions, as they have in other settings from Dubuque to Brooklyn to San Francisco. I answer all of them as best as I can, telling them that whatever their struggles are, they do get better. Maybe it sounds trite, but I sincerely believe it as long as kids have love and support.

We have to do better. I have to do better. Hanging out at an Oscar party with Lady Gaga is nice, and I truly appreciate her public support of my transition. Hanging out in private with kids needing support is more rewarding.

Last year I gave out my cell number at church to a teenager struggling with gender dysphoria and communicating with parents who had trouble dealing with it. I told him to call or text me, and he does.

I met at my house for several hours with a mother and her trans teen daughter who had flown out from New Jersey. I invited a trans woman I have gotten to know named Ella, who transitioned as a senior in high school only a few years earlier. I wanted the daughter to see that Ella came out thriving on the other side, and now the two of them follow each other on social media.

As a parent I also can identify with the fears of the mom, not simply in terms of acceptance of her daughter in school and the community, but the impact transition had on their own relationship. I remember someone asking me one day how I would handle it if one of my children had transitioned as a teenager. Despite my own transition, I know I would have had anxiety, this feeling of my daughter or son becoming someone I no longer know. But no matter how difficult it would be for me, I would never stand in the way of any of my children. The mom felt relief when I related to her that her fears are common for any parent.

I have received thousands of letters. Many thank me for going public with my story and how it inspired them to transition. Some have told me they were contemplating suicide and decided not to because of my willingness to be so open.

About a year ago I was connected to a transgender woman from South Dakota who was convinced she would not be able to find work because of the climate of the state: legislation restricting bathroom use in schools by transgender teens was passed until a veto by the governor. Other anti-LGBTQ legislation had been proposed as well. She was right to think the atmosphere was toxic:

Nobody will hire me.

We spoke on the phone at least a dozen times. I asked her what her interests were, and she said she loved doing makeup. Because of my association with MAC Cosmetics,

I told her to see if there was a retail store in the state and I would call the company to make sure she got hired. There wasn't one, so I urged her to try a department store. She was terrified when she went in to apply. She got a job and afterward sent me a video of her crying, she was so joyful.

None of this makes me remotely special.

Only human.

Focusing on the issues is enormously important. But when I first met with the trans women who would become a part of my reality television show on E!, *I Am Cait*, and talked about all the lives we had to save, I remember Chandi Moore saying something I will never forget. Chandi has spent years working with trans and gender nonconforming kids at Children's Hospital Los Angeles in the program Brave Leaders Unified to Strengthen our Health (BLUSH). As I was talking she interrupted me, which is typical of Chandi when there is something that needs to be said.

You can't save every soul, but you can save one soul at a time.

It sunk in that you can talk about the big issues as much as you want, and that's important, but you also have to go one-on-one on a personal level. I can only do so much. I obviously cannot prevent every suicide, as much as I wish I could. But I also know how crucial it is to reach out to individuals, which is why I do it. I hope others in a position to do the same will reach out as well. If we all save one soul at a time, then collectively we will save thousands.

* * *

I watch those balloons released into the sky on that strip of beach. I leave feeling not just sadness but anger that this could have been prevented if our society would begin to pride itself on acceptance instead of rejection, inclusion instead of exclusion. Stop making us outcasts. We are a vibrant and diverse community.

I think of Kyler Prescott slumped in the bathroom. I think of his mother finding him. I think of the poem he wrote. Not only was it unusually haunting and beautiful for a fourteen-year-old; it also captured the exact same feeling I had when I looked into the mirror and for so long saw someone I did not recognize. It captured the struggle in all of us.

> *My mirror does not define me:*
> *Not the stranger that looks back at me*
> *Not the smooth face that belongs to someone else*
> *Not the eyes that gleam with sadness*
> *When I look for him and can only see her.*
> *My body does not define me:*
> *Not the slim shoulders that will not change*
> *Not the hips that give me away*
> *Not the chest I can't stand to look at*
> *When I look for him and can only see her.*
> *My clothes do not define me:*
> *Not the shirt and jeans*

That would look so perfect on him
But I know would never fit me
When I look for him and can only find her.
And I've been looking for him for years,
But I seem to grow farther away from him
With each passing day.

—ᴡ—

Chapter Two

Just Drop the Damn Ski

It is gym class at my elementary school in Tarrytown. The coach has set up a series of cones in the parking lot. Everybody is going to be timed.

Let's get in there and see what we can do.

I have never gone out for a team sport in school. I have no idea of my skill level. Frankly, I'm not very competitive. I do things because they are fun and come naturally, and this seems like fun to me.

Each of us runs around the orange cones, the coach poised with his stopwatch. He jots down all the times. He looks at me. Classmates who have never given me the slightest attention are patting me on the back. The coach's stopwatch confirms it.

I'm the fastest kid in the entire school!

So maybe there is an outlet for success for me. And it's not just success as I move up the sports ladder. What better way to prove masculinity? What better way to get rid of this *thing*? Athletes don't try on women's clothing.

Athletes don't walk around the block in a scarf. Athletes parade their private parts in the locker room. We are the titans.

Sports is the perfect cover in the 1960s, the kingdom of the male, specifically the white male (and it is still the perfect cover now). There is no Title Nine, providing equality for men and women in sports. Integration in college sports is slow and hesitant. As for issues of gender or sexuality, sports are once again the perfect protection. An openly transgender athlete in the 1960s? It is still an underground network: express yourself and you run the risk of being harassed or arrested. Stonewall, the watershed event in the history of the LGBTQ movement, when members reacted violently to a police raid of the Stonewall Inn in New York, would not take place until 1969, when I was in college. The raid targets trans women in standard police procedure of the era: because of a New York City criminal statute requiring three articles of gender-appropriate clothing, police take into custody those deemed in violation, whereupon they would either feel them up or make them undress to determine their gender and whether the three-article rule is being followed.

It will not be until 1975 when I am twenty-six that Dave Kopay, a journeyman National Football League running back for nine seasons, will tell the *Washington Star* that he is homosexual after a series in the paper quotes an anonymous gay football player whom Kopay recognizes as someone he once slept with. And that is two years after his retirement, since going public while playing would have been career suicide. (Even today there are no openly gay athletes actively playing in either Major League Baseball or the National Football League. Professional female athletes have been far more open about their sexual preference, an indication that the environment is far less hostile, and the athletes are more honest and celebratory of themselves.)

I have found my calling because of that race in fifth grade.

When I move up to junior high, word is out that I'm fast, and a couple of older kids come up to me one day.

So you're fast, huh?

I guess.

Let's see what you got. Let's race.

I am fast. But I'm not stupid.

I run.

Home.

As a kid dealing with all these confusing feelings, nothing makes me feel better about myself than going out on the football field and clocking someone. It isn't just aggression but an expression of one's ego—you feel dominant over something and can never let go of it. I was never naturally a great athlete. But as I get older and see how my drive to perform and outwork all the other athletes develops, the decathlon becomes more important to me. While this drive obviously comes from a sense of competition, it also comes from a place of having to constantly purge what is going round and round inside, that the only way to fight inferiority is with superiority.

Aware of the status that athletics bestows, I play popular team sports such as football and basketball at Sleepy Hollow High School in Tarrytown. I like them. They are *fun*. But I prefer situations where I rely on myself. I want to be in control of my destiny, maybe because so much of my life is about control.

If I win, I did it. If I lose, it is my fault. I get to walk away by myself. I don't have to commiserate with teammates or for that matter celebrate with them. I am a loner, inevitable for anyone who carries inside the secret of themselves they cannot share. I am friendly but still aloof, still at arm's length from everyone else. Because I am good at what I do, people leave me alone. I have friends on the football and basketball teams, but I don't hang with them. People like me, probably because my first car is a 1954 Cadillac hearse (not kidding) and I am able to pack twenty-four of my high school compatriots into the casket compartment one night (still not kidding).

I don't want people to know who I am, what I think about, and what I grapple with. If anything I act a little goofy because it puts me further above the fray, the Jenner kid who marches to his own tune. It is not that I cannot feel, but I am scared to. All feelings do is stir up conflict within me. I am on the fringe because I like being on the fringe. It's safer, easier, better.

The loner.

The sport I like the most is track and field. And the event I like the most within track and field is the pole vault. I pick it up as a freshman in high school. I like the freedom and the spiraling aloneness. There is nothing like running down a narrow lane with a long pole and planting it like a staff into the indentation, arcing in a slow curve before you spring to get over the top. I like that it involves mind and body and lessens the inner turmoil. My dad builds a pole vault pit in the backyard so I can practice. I ultimately become the Connecticut state champion in high school and two-time MVP of the track team.

In addition to school-based sports, my dad is looking for an activity that the entire family can participate in on the weekends.

He chooses waterskiing, so he buys a boat. We all go out on Candlewood Lake in Connecticut. I am scared, or maybe more accurately I'm afraid of embarrassment that will only add to my already thick layer of insecurity. I have been embarrassed enough as a child. My dad knows me better than I do and admires my athletic skills more than I do, because I don't think there is anything particularly special about me. I'm just a confused kid trying to get by. He knows about the dyslexia, but he doesn't know I like Mom's closet and how that is affecting my self-image as well. And he will never know. *Ever.* I will never tell him. He will never catch me. That can never happen. *Ever.* Plus it's just some weird thing I like for the time being. It will pass, so there is no point in ever mentioning it to anyone.

One of his favorite routines on Candlewood Lake is the so-called whip technique: he takes the boat in a circle, the effect of which makes the skier go faster and faster because of the centripetal force created. I scream at him the first time he does that to me at the age of ten or eleven. He keeps on doing it, and I scream some more. My sister Pam picks it up quickly, which only makes matters worse. Until it finally begins to click. Then he wants me to drop one of my skis so I'm only skimming the water on one ski, and here we go again. I won't do it. I can't do it. I'm just getting used to two skis.

Please, Dad, don't make me try. I can't handle the failure. I have had enough of those in my life. I'm already weird enough. I feel it every day. Please, Dad, don't add to it.

He won't let go.

Just drop the damn ski.

Okay, I'll do it. Just don't say it anymore.

Just drop the damn ski.

Okay, I said I would do it!

Just drop the damn ski.

I take the chance. I do it.

I feel exhilaration afterward. I go on in my middle and late teens to win the Eastern States waterskiing championship three times. The victories are sweet, but what I really learn from waterskiing, thanks to my dad, is the humility that will carry through the rest of my life. His credo is simple: actions speak for themselves, not speaking.

Let everyone else go out there and perform, then you do it without a word. Don't even tell them you can ski. Let them figure it out for themselves once you're done.

High school is about other things besides sports, of course. I suppose it's about grades, although my only academic interest is in that C average so I can remain eligible. There is also dating and sex, which go hand-in-hand with being a big man on campus.

I am a star on the football team, the most popular sport in high school. So going out with girls is the thing to do. But I am shy and awkward and date only a handful, none with lasting consequences. As for sex, guys talk about it nonstop, so I feel I have to go in that direction. Because I both put women on a pedestal and envy them, I am not a stereotypic aggressive male jock. I prefer being on the bottom instead of the top, which in the context of a suburban town in the 1960s is heresy. So I take the top bunk, so to speak, and do my best.

I have sex with my first girl when I am a senior at Newtown High School in Sandy Hook, Connecticut, where we moved to in my junior year. It takes place in the backseat of my mom's black Ford Falcon station wagon. I'm ever the romantic. The only thing I remember with perfect clarity is that she is a lot smarter than I am. I do it because I am curious, and there is a definite attraction.

And maybe I do it out of obligation to maintain appearances. Everybody in high school knows who has slept with whom, and this is helpful to me in maintaining cover.

Unlike many athletes I will get to know in later life after high school, I do not keep a running journal in my head of conquests. It would be a very short scrapbook if I did.

I don't have the appetite for it, which is why the public's obsession over my sex life now, whether I will or won't, is annoying to me. It hearkens back to this endless misperception that men and women transition because of their sexual preference and desires. They endlessly wonder if a man becomes a woman and still enjoys sex with women, what does that make her? Who the hell cares? Why must labels be attached to everything? My preference has not changed now that I have transitioned. Why would it? I have always enjoyed women. Not that I think of it a lot. Of the most important things in my life, sex is beyond the bottom; it has been that way for a long time. A future female companion? Yes, I do think about that. A future female sexual companion? Not happening, at least for now, and perhaps not ever.

A future male sexual companion? I have never had the inclination. But maybe that attitude might possibly change if I have the Final Surgery. Maybe removing the last physical appendage of my maleness, or more precisely, maleness as defined by the medical establishment, will make me feel differently. Some would argue that there is no good reason to have gender-affirming surgery as a trans woman unless you are intent on having sex with men. For me the reason to do it is different: feeling as authentic as I possibly can.

Mostly I float through high school. I have no burning ambition in sports, maybe because I have yet to find the right event that plays into my versatility. I am good in the pole vault but not competitive on a national level. The decathlon? At this point it's just another word I have difficulty spelling. Unlike so many great athletes who come out of the crib ready to go, I am not. I like to win, but competition does not ooze from every pore. I maintain that happy-go-lucky core, so much so that when I make all-county in track and the local paper wants to take a picture of me and other athletes honored, I forget to bring my track shoes and appear in loafers.

If there was ever an athlete *not* destined for greatness, it was me. I do have self-discipline. I am able to shut things out, including my gender issues. They are always there, but in high school they are mostly in check. I still cross-dress when I can. But getting the opportunity is hard, although I have moved up to Pam's clothing since Mom's is now way too small. Just as I admire women, I am also jealous of them. I feel that bubbling inside me, not because of the way they look but because of how comfortable they seem and knowing I will never be able to feel that way. Just as I see how comfortable men are and knowing I will never feel that way, either. I feel as if I am of no gender, trapped in the worst place to be: the middle.

I remember Ella (she will become a regular on *I Am Cait*) telling me of her experience in high school, how she made no effort to blend in and just be one of the crowd. She wore her hair purple. She sometimes wore dresses. She made it clear that she was shedding her skin as a boy. She celebrated herself regardless of what other students thought.

I so admired Ella's fearlessness. I so admired her acceptance of her true gender identity not as a curse but as a blessing and liberation. I wonder sometimes why I didn't do that in high school, just say screw it and set myself free. There were obvious reasons—the tenor of the times, the social conservatism not only of my immediate environment but of America as a whole. I would have been sent to shrinks who still believed that gender dysphoria, just like homosexuality, was a disease that could be cured using such barbaric methods as electric shock or inducing vomiting while showing the "patient" homoerotic images. I certainly would not have been able to play any sports. I probably would have been thrown out of school. But perhaps it was all more basic than that.

I just didn't have the courage. That's what took me so long.

I only wanted to blend in.

As I near graduation from Newtown High, the only definite plan I have is to continue my education, which will also grant me a college deferment from the Vietnam War draft. Although I was the MVP of every sport

I played at Newtown High for the five semesters I was there (basketball, football, and track), I am not heavily recruited.

The only place I get any real interest from is Graceland College in Lamoni, Iowa. I am not interested in Graceland. I know nothing about Iowa except that it is flat and cold in the winter. The school is affiliated with the Reorganized Church of Jesus Christ of Latter Day Saints—known today as the Community of Christ—and I don't know anything about the religion except that it's a mouthful.

I have never gone west of Ohio. I have been on an airplane only once in my life. New York City might as well be on the dark side of the moon. I have no hippie tendencies. I am straight and narrow and following in the conservatism of my parents. So my plan is to continue living at home after high school to keep my expenses down, go to a junior college nearby to get my grades up so I can attend a four-year school, and work for my dad's tree business on the weekends to make a little money. I am kind of aimless, to tell the truth. Maybe a career in mechanical drawing. I don't really know.

I have just attended the first day of classes at junior college when I get a call from L.D. Weldon, the athletic director and track coach at Graceland.

Hello?

Can you be out here tomorrow to play football?

Who is this?

L.D. Weldon. I coach at Graceland.

I don't know.

Well, the quarterback we recruited from a junior college is a credit short, so he isn't eligible, and we only have one back-up quarterback, so we need somebody else.

Okay.

Football is still fun to me.

Call me back tomorrow and I'll give you an answer.

I talk to my parents that night. They cannot afford to send me to college, so I go to the bank the next day and arrange for a student loan since the scholarship is only partial. Weldon calls me and I tell him my decision.

Okay, I'll be there tomorrow.

He hangs up.

—◠—

July 15, 2015

"Please, God, don't let me trip"

I am making my first public appearance as Caitlyn in Los Angeles.

I am wearing a white Donatella Versace evening gown custom-made by the designer. I have not met her personally, but she has sent emissaries on several occasions to make sure the fit is right. Only one of them speaks English, but if I have learned anything from *Keeping Up with the Kardashians*, it is that the language of fashion is universal.

I want to look sleek and gorgeous. Scratch that: I *need* to look sleek and gorgeous. If I come onstage looking like anything less, the behind-my-back ridicule, which you can always hear anyway, will be merciless. If anybody wants to know what that kind of savage mockery feels like, how it affects your self-image at a moment in your life where your self-image is still a blur, hire a swarm of paparazzi and ask them to chase you around from the time you get up in the morning until the time you go to bed at night for the next ten years of your life.

Gowns are tricky when you are not used to them. You can step on the hem and go flying. Good thing I switched into a pair of shoes with a shorter heel to minimize the risk. Actually, since you cannot see the shoes at all, I should have worn a pair of my old shot-put shoes for extra precaution.

Please, God, you have made my life confusing enough already.

Please, God, don't let me trip.

It is all I can think about, tripping when it's time to walk up the small set of stairs to the stage of the Microsoft Theater in Los Angeles to accept one of the most prestigious and meaningful awards in sports.

If I trip, it becomes a bigger picture than the one Annie Leibovitz took of me in a cream-colored bustier for the cover of *Vanity Fair* a month and a half prior. Tripping is not the way I want to be remembered. Tripping would give the paparazzi way too much satisfaction. Social media would hit the jackpot.

I also have a great deal to say. It is an important moment for me, maybe the most important in my life besides the birth of my children. The final day of the decathlon in Montreal, when I either would win the gold medal and have something to show for those twelve years of training or not win the gold medal and go home a nobody with nothing to show for those twelve years of training, pales in comparison. This is my life, not a sporting event.

The trans community already has issues with me, and

I've only reached my four-month anniversary. They are fabulous, but some can be tough and critical, frustrating and debilitating at times. I am already hearing I am not "representative" of the community. I certainly won't dispute that, although such judgment strikes me as hostile and exclusionary and counterproductive to our collective cause, since much of our fight is to get society to remove such meaningless labels as *representative*. We are all in this together, or at least we should be.

But tonight, like it or not, I am the face of the transgender community to millions who have never seen a trans woman or man in their lives. The first impression is often the lasting impression. If I screw this up, I will set back the movement. I will have squandered a rare opportunity on behalf of all of us who are different and should be celebrated for it, not forced underground.

Controversy has begun well before the annual ESPY award ceremony at which I will receive the Arthur Ashe Courage Award, named for the great and gracious tennis star who died of AIDS in 1993. I have been to the ESPYs, ESPN's version of the Academy Awards for sports, many times. It is a huge honor, given my respect for Ashe and others who have won the award in the past: Muhammad Ali, Billie Jean King, Tommie Smith, John Carlos, Nelson Mandela, Robin Roberts.

That's the simple part.

The fact that this will be Caitlyn's first public appearance is terrifying enough. Now add to it that it's an appearance before the world of sports, from which I came. Then add to it the millions watching on television. Do I think I deserve it? Absolutely not. But nobody would turn down such an honor.

I am also dealing with a rumor that I was the one who came up with the idea. The scenario goes that in return for giving ABC's Diane Sawyer an exclusive two-hour interview on *20/20* in April 2015 in which I publicly announced my intent to transition, I insisted on receiving the Arthur Ashe award at the ESPYs as a quid pro quo. The rumor was fed by the fact that the same company, Disney, owns ABC and ESPN. It is one hundred percent wrong, complete bullshit. There is no other appropriate word. The actual interview took place months before I was told I would be receiving the Arthur Ashe award. But like so many false rumors today, it has jumped beyond the tabloids into such mainstream media as the *Los Angeles Times*. You would think they might like to check first given their holier-than-thou reputations. In today's world?

Be serious.

So right at the beginning there has been negative spin in some corners. Then come several prominent figures in sports saying I do not deserve the award. One of them is Frank Deford, a renowned writer for *Sports Illustrated* and an NPR commentator. It was Deford who wrote the cover story on me in the August 9, 1976, issue of the magazine after I won the decathlon:

Jenner has an almost mystical ability to divine his own limits, and those who have been with him at meets say that by studying his opponents as the events go by, he can perceive their exact capabilities that day. Montreal, he felt, was his "destiny."

Almost forty years later, the tenor is different:

Courage is usually involved with overcoming something. Caitlyn Jenner is being forthright and honest, but this is something that she wanted, and she has a fallback position—a reality show, fame and lots of money. There's not a great deal of risk involved in the same way that someone who worked down at the body shop would experience. Bruce Jenner had a good idea that he wasn't going to lose by doing this; his family is in support of him.

Deford and I are in agreement that there is no particular courage in my transition. As for overcoming something, the only thing I overcame was knowing I was in the wrong gender for most of my life and being too scared to truly deal with it. I was in the public eye and worried about ridicule and scorn and hatred and condemnation and what the Frank Defords of the world would think in the context of the 1980s if I showed up for some rubber-chicken sports award dinner in a skirt and pardoned myself to go to the ladies room, assuming I would be allowed into the ladies room, to freshen up.

As for the support of my family, they have all been incredible. More than incredible. But it has only been a little more than a month since I publicly became Caitlyn, and every day I wonder what all my children from my three marriages really think, whether they do truly accept me and can still call me Dad as if it still has meaning or instead look at me like some quasi-stranger who is selfish to do this at such a late stage in life. It is not a reflection upon them but upon me, the fear of acceptance I now feel no matter how outwardly effusive that acceptance has been, waking up in the morning and thinking about gender and the decisions I have made and going to bed thinking the very same things.

As Caitlyn instead of Bruce, I am now a public person no longer in the private shadow. That does things to your head. Doubt—different from regret because I have no regret—is a universal sensation among virtually every man and woman after initially transitioning. Once you do so you never go back. Never. And every relationship you have will change either because it has changed or you think it has changed. All of which is a way of saying that in my mind at least there is a lot on the line—my relationship with my family and the rest of my life.

The other vocal critic is NBC sportscaster and commentator Bob Costas. Speaking on the *Dan Patrick Show*, Costas says he wishes me:

all the happiness in the world and all the peace of mind in the world...However, it strikes me that awarding the Arthur Ashe Award to Caitlyn Jenner is just a crass exploitation play—it's a tabloid play.

In the broad world of sports, I'm pretty sure they could've found someone—and this is not anything against Caitlyn Jenner—who was much closer to [being] actively involved in sports, who would've been deserving of what the award represents.

Costas is an excellent sportscaster and commentator. I know how hard it is, having done it. He insists it is not a personal attack on me, and I believe Costas, but it sure sounds like one, the obvious implication being that I am not worthy of the award. There have also been recipients like me, who at the time of receiving the honor had performed at their peak much earlier.

If he and Deford want to see what it's like to be a transgender woman or man—even one as privileged as me—they should transition. I will be happy to help them shop. Sensible heels for Deford since he's tall. Stilettos for Costas since he is rather diminutive.

For most of the ceremony I am in a suite at the Ritz-Carlton hotel across the street. I don't watch on television, because it will only make me more nervous. About fifteen to twenty minutes before my appearance, I exit the hotel from the back and go directly into the theater so no one can see me. They put me in a small private room and I practice the speech for what seems the millionth time, what to emphasize, getting the beats right, figuring out the pacing, not garbling or tripping over words. I feel good, but there is still the issue of the steps to the stage: the anticipation is a little like when I ran my weakest event at the Games, the 110-meter hurdles, but at least I finished even with a few missteps.

I have often used a Booker T. Washington paraphrase: "success is not measured by heights obtained but by obstacles overcome." If there is a moment to invoke it, this is it.

Abby Wambach, a forward on the United States women's soccer team that just won the World Cup, is introducing me. I meet her for the first time backstage.

Hi.

Hi.

A little brief, but there is something weighing on me.

When I come up the stairs to the stage, you have to help me. I cannot trip. Make sure I don't have any problems.

Okay, I'll get you up the stairs.

I need a hand.

Abby is in a tuxedo and I am in my gown. The symbolism of that is sublime, not to mention a photo-op too good to be wasted, no better way to visually show how far sports has come in terms of diversity (with a long way still to go).

When we get up there, assuming there are no disasters, I want us to turn and hold hands and take a little bow.

See, always thinking whatever the pressure.

They bring me to the side of the stage. I can peek out and see that the place is pretty much packed.

Here we go...

I make eye contact with a woman in the audience. She gives me a huge smile and a thumbs-up.

Maybe the reaction will be okay.

At the commercial break there is the weird dance of audience members leaving and seat fillers taking their place. I sneak into the audience. I see Diane Sawyer. Had the interview not so accurately depicted what my life had been like up until transition, I probably would be in Antarctica sharing my tale of deceit and destruction with the penguins. I grab her hand and say to her:

This is all your fault.

I know this is supposed to be all very serious. But I can't be. It has never been my style. Humor is always the best deflection.

I am sitting in the audience when a video comes on showing the cavalcade of my life. I saw it two days earlier. It is elegant and tasteful, and I cried when I first saw it. The juxtaposition of Bruce and Caitlyn is shocking even to me. How could one become the other and the other become the one? I know that Caitlyn was my gender identity at birth, waiting for the right moment to subsume Bruce. But sometimes answers don't quite answer it. As I have said to myself many times,

I have had a most fascinating life.

I can't watch it now. It will make me emotional again, and I won't be able to give my speech.

Abby calls my name to come to the stage. I am next to my mother in the audience, the last person I told of my transition and the hardest to tell, which is why I waited so long. She is eighty-nine, and it just isn't so easy to have your son call up on what seems to be a normal day in Lewiston, Idaho, and have him tell you, *Oh, I forgot to mention, Mom. I'm becoming a woman.*

It wasn't quite framed like that. But it had the same impact. There is no right way to begin a conversation like that. My mother has been remarkably understanding and supportive, although she readily admits to a little shot of something to make my womanhood go down easier.

I leave my seat. As I get nearer to those little steps, I go past the rows on the left where my children are sitting. It is the first time in roughly twenty years they have all been together, not since the 1990s when Kris and I were first married and they were kids who adored each other just as Kris and I adored each other. There are many reasons for why our extended family fell apart, but at the root of it was my failure as a father. On too many occasions I let my relationship to the so-called Jenner children from my first two marriages—Burt and Cassandra and Brandon and Brody—slip away. So it is beautiful to see all my family together again, just as it is also bittersweet. I know it is only a moment, one that doesn't even last to the after-party.

Abby gives me a hand as promised.

I do not trip up the stairs.

We do our pirouette to the delight of the cameras.

Now all I have to do is give the speech of my life.

I try not to look at the audience. There are dozens of sports legends assembled. They are my peers. I can't avoid seeing LeBron James and Brett Favre sitting in the front row. I wonder what the hell they are thinking. I always wonder what everyone is *really* thinking underneath the surface of being nice to me. Are they just saying things to please me but don't really believe a word? Are they lying? I sometimes wish there was someone who could interview them privately, get down their real thoughts as opposed to celebrity cocktail party kissy-face chatter. Do they really think it's great? Or do they really think the whole thing is very *very* weird?

Is the gown too much, however perfectly executed? Should I have shown up in my Olympic tracksuit? LeBron is a sharp dresser, but Favre often looks as if he just came out of a barn. So I think I have better odds with LeBron. I imagine he digs the Versace label, although maybe not in this particular style. Plus he is even taller than I am and far more muscled.

Out of the hundreds I have given in my life, never have I written out an entire speech. At most I jot down highlights. I don't like reading a speech, because it sounds like reading a speech. But this is different. I collaborate with a writer, which I also have never done before. His name is Aaron Cohen, and we spend several sessions together where I give him my ideas of what I want to say and he helps shape them. Then we get it down on paper. I need to know exactly what I am going to say here. I cannot riff, which I sometimes do (actually, I do it a lot), and suddenly veer off into unwanted territory.

I am also going to use a teleprompter. But because I tend to read slowly, I have hated them since my days as a broadcaster for ABC and NBC in the 1970s and 1980s. I need to practice, so I discover an application on my iPad that simulates one down to the size of the letters and the speed. I set the iPad on the cushion of a high kitchen chair and then read aloud as it scrolls through the words. I do this dozens of times until I have it down perfectly.

But now that the moment has come...

I feel myself traveling back to fourth grade in Tarrytown, sitting there scared to death with sweaty palms as the teacher walks down the aisle like a prison guard looking for the next victim to read aloud. I can hear the snickers of classmates as I stumble, and I have just gotten used to the fact that it's Bruce and Bruce is stupid. My elementary school years can be easily summed up: first one picked for dodgeball, first one to sit down in the spelling bee.

I have to fight through it, so I do. I am good at conquering adversity. I did it all my life, although never in a situation such as this.

I no longer see LeBron James or Brett Favre. I no longer see my children or my mother. Once again I don't see anyone, almost as if someone else is giving the speech and I, too, am a curious observer.

The words come out:

All across this country, right now, all across the world, at this very moment, there are young people coming to terms with being transgender. They're learning that they're different, and they are trying to figure out how to handle that, on top of every other problem that a teenager has. They're getting bullied, they're getting beaten up, they're getting murdered, and they're committing suicide. The numbers are staggering, but they are the reality of what it is like to be trans today.

If there is one thing I do know about my life, it is the power of spotlight. Sometimes it gets overwhelming, but with attention comes responsibility. As a group, as athletes, how you conduct your lives, what you say, what you do is absorbed and observed by millions of people, especially young people.

I know I'm clear with my responsibility going forward, to tell my story the right way, for me to keep learning, to reshape the landscape of how trans issues are viewed, how trans people are treated. And then more broadly to promote a very simple idea: accepting people for who they are. Accepting people's differences.

This transition has been harder on me than anything I could imagine. And that's the case for so many others besides me. For that reason alone, trans people deserve something vital. They deserve your respect. And from that respect comes a more compassionate community, a more empathetic society, and a better world for all of us.

I get a standing ovation louder in my mind than the roars in the Olympic stadium when I finished the 1,500-meter run to win the decathlon. It certainly is more important.

I didn't trip after all.

—⚡—

Chapter Three

Just Take It

L.D. Weldon is picking me up at the airport in Des Moines. I don't even know what he looks like. He doesn't know what I look like. How are we going to find each other?

I get off the plane and walk down the stairs. I go into the terminal and look around and feel a little bit like that book about the ducklings in Boston thinking everyone is their mother.

Are you my coach?

Suddenly out of the crowd comes a hand.

Jenner?

Yeah.

Hi, nice to meet you. L.D. Weldon, Graceland College.

How did you know it was me?

I can always spot an athlete.

That's kind of cool.

Get your bags, Jenner.

I only have two of them. We throw them into the

backseat of Weldon's car for the seventy-five-mile drive to Lamoni.

I can't pinpoint his age, but it's obvious his days as a Chippendale—if he ever had them and I kind of doubt he did—are behind him. He has one hand stretched over the back of the seat and the other hand on the steering wheel. He's looking at me while he's driving and he's also talking nonstop. He's also going about ninety miles an hour.

It is an amazing feat unless you are next to him and just hoping not to die before you even see the college.

L.D. had built a few apartments in a back alley of Lamoni to house Graceland athletes so they could save some money. Anything that is free is a good thing, so I wasn't about to complain. But I am not sure it would be fair to call them apartments. The entrance is in back through a door with cracks in it so huge you can literally see through it. And when the cold wind whistles through Lamoni, it is like sleeping on the surface of a skating rink. Behind a second door are four or five rooms and a single bathroom. It looks as if L.D. has converted a storage area, and my room is barely big enough to contain my six-foot-two frame. At least there is new paneling.

I unpack, which takes about two seconds—underwear, socks, a few pairs of pants, a thin jacket that soon proves useless in the weather.

I go to my first football practice. Although I have played quarterback in high school, I have also played a lot of other positions—running back, a little receiver. On defense I play safety, and it is my best position. It's a lot more satisfying to hit than to get hit. I can throw the ball fifty to sixty yards without much problem. The greater question is *where* exactly I throw it. Receivers, in my experience, are often fleeting objects that suddenly disappear.

But they need a backup quarterback, so tag, I am it. I take a few practice snaps and then I drop back to pass and I throw a perfect bullet—right into the hands of Bob Hutchins, who goes both ways at running back and safety and is the star of the team, for an interception. Hutchins is sailing down the sidelines. I angle toward him and I am quick and I get a clear shot and I nail him.

An assistant coach named Bill Dudek comes running over.

Oh my God. You're a defensive player! Change his shirt!

So I am moved to safety, a position that much better suits me. I adapt easily to Graceland. My only goal is just to fit in. I am a big man on campus, but a minor one. There is no obligation to show sexual prowess.

We are playing Tarkio. They line up to punt. I am a little bit behind the line, almost like a linebacker. We put a cross-block on to free the middle, and I sail through untouched. I have a perfect dot shot. I am hell-bent. But as I spring up to block the kick my right knee is extended, and one of their players hits me square on in the middle of it. I limp off the field, and I have the sensation that my career in sports might be over. I try to rehab it, but it goes out a second time during a game of catch, and I know I have to do something.

I have suffered medial collateral ligament damage and undergo an operation on January 2, 1969, in Danbury, Connecticut, by Dr. Robert Fornshell. He opens up the knee and puts a staple in to help stabilize it. He wishes me good luck. (I received a wonderful letter from him after the 1976 Olympics in which he said that most of his patients were now dead, so it was nice to see one who was still living and doing well. I, too, was happy about that.)

My knee is placed in a cast for six weeks, and I have already missed four weeks of the second semester when I return to Graceland. I can't run track, so instead I have to watch everyone else. I am just trying to walk since my knee is horribly stiff from being in a cast for so long. L.D. does most of the rehab—massaging, cold treatments, hot treatments. I lay on a trainer's table and he forces my leg down and it hurts like nothing has ever hurt before and L.D., being L.D., voices his sympathy in a distinct way:

Just take it.

I was used to the mantra because I had often whispered it to myself whenever my gender issues intensified.

Just take it.

Freshman year becomes a disaster: I have no motivation to stay in school when I'm deprived of the outlet of sports. The only good thing about my knee surgery is that I will most likely flunk the physical if I'm drafted.

I am a wanderer once again, aimless in ambition or pursuit, and already a discernible pattern has emerged— the less focused I am, the less I can grab on to something with all my conscious might, the more my gender confusion comes to the surface. I buy a pair of bell-bottom pants, the current style. They excite me with the tight buttocks and pant legs. They are form fitting, or as form fitting as any men's clothing ever gets. I get a rush, an excitement in wearing them. It's a silly pair of pants, but that's how desperate I am to feel something, anything. That's how bottled up I am, starved for any crumb of what I increasingly know is my true gender.

By now I always have the urge to be myself and cross-dress. But as a student at Graceland I have no privacy. Students and professors are always coming and going, and I still don't fully know what is going on inside me except for my conviction that something is terribly wrong with me. Maybe I am really screwed up. Please just let it be a phase, because if it isn't, I never want to face it.

I go back home after my freshman year and work for my dad again. I am thinking more and more that I don't want to return to college, particularly after I am offered a job at Cypress Gardens, the best waterskiing show in the United States and maybe the world, headquartered in Winter Haven, Florida. I'm now nineteen, so living in Florida and waterskiing for a living does sound pretty good to me.

In the back of my mind I am also thinking about the decathlon, even though I have never participated in one. L.D. has a reputation for training Olympic-caliber decathletes.

I was versatile in high school. My best sport is still the pole vault, even if in my first attempt ever I cleared the height by a mile, then promptly hit the crossbar smack in the face and cut myself. But I was on crappy teams, and the coach would turn to me and ask:

Hey, can you long jump?

Yeah, why not?

Can you high jump?

Yeah, why not?

Can you run out and get me a coffee before the next event cream and extra sugar?

Yeah, why not?

I was always a very helpful person.

Even when I was a freshman L.D. had been planting whispers in my ear about the decathlon. So now I wonder if the best course is to return to work for my father and go back to Graceland in the fall of 1969.

I am staying in Richmond, Virginia, competing in a waterskiing tournament. I have to make a decision. Waterskiing in Florida or going back to college and training for something in which there is no guarantee of success.

I get into my car, a 1956 Ford Fairlane convertible (I wish I had kept that car rather than the accordion). I'm headed to interstate 95 with two choices—head north toward home and college, or head south to Florida. I'm almost at the on-ramps, and I still have not made up my mind. I'm in the right-hand lane to turn north. A car pulls up in the left-hand lane to turn south. If I want to go south, I have to either sharply apply the brakes or try to speed around it. The ramp for I-95 north is wide open, not another car on the road.

I head north.

There are many places in life where you see these crossroads—everybody has them, although usually not in such a literal sense. At the time it doesn't seem like that big of a decision, but then you look back at it and think, *Oh my God, what if I had turned left there?*

My entire life would have been different.

I would not have won the Olympics. For better or worse I would not have become an American hero. I would not have gotten lucrative endorsements from major corporations. I would not have had fame and celebrity. I would have been largely anonymous. But I also would have been free of expectation. I would have been far more free to be my authentic self: no one outside of family and a few close friends would have noticed or cared. By going right I certainly prospered in a certain sense. By not going left I failed to prosper at all where it counts the most, to celebrate my difference instead of driving away from it.

After my return to Graceland in 1969 for my sophomore year, L.D. mercilessly bends my ear even more about the decathlon. In my heart I still see the kid who had been the dimwitted dyslexic growing up and loved burying himself in his mother's closet. L.D. thinks that I have just enough athletic skill to be good. Because he later says that I am not close to the best pure athlete he ever coached.

He ranks me fifth. Fifth? *Fifth?* Had L.D. ever told me that, I probably would have quit, which is why he never told me. But he also later said that when it came to the combination of athleticism and desire, there was no equal. I did have more drive than anyone else. I also had more to prove, maybe because I had more to hide.

L.D. becomes a father figure, not as a replacement for my own father but as an extension of him—wheedling, needling, pushing me to overcome fear, the hovering cloud that for all my outward jock-walk bullshit I am neither strong nor particularly deserving of being strong.

Just drop the damn ski...

L.D. doesn't leave me alone, talking nonstop in his porkpie hat and oval-rimmed black glasses and coat and narrow tie—for some reason he reminds me of a bobblehead—talking more than any person I have ever met in my life (except perhaps for me).

It begins to make some sense. Sometimes in my head I jot down the number of total points I think I could register in the decathlon, even though there are some events I have never even competed in. It adds up to 7,000, which would be a school record on my first try. I particularly like the number of events. Ten. *Ten different events.* Ten events to train in any day or every day for as many days as you want: the 100 meters, the long jump, the shot put, the high jump, the 400 meters, the 110-meter hurdles, the discus, the pole vault, the javelin, the 1,500 meters, in this exact order. You can get swallowed up in that. You can lose yourself in that. Whatever thoughts you have inside don't go away, but they do go numb. The Olympics? Who knows? In finding the drive to do something unimaginable, I am also finding the drive not to do something unimaginable.

The Grand Diversion.

I go home for winter break, and for the first time in my life see a sustained pathway. I am working for my dad to make a little money, and one day there is an emergency that brings me back to my other reality in which it's time to stop the fantasy and get to work.

The top of a tree on Bantam Lake in Connecticut has broken off. It is hanging on the limb below and has to be removed before it falls onto several high-tension electrical wires. A co-worker and I drive out to the site. It is about zero degrees outside with a good twenty-mile-per-hour wind whipping off the lake.

The treetop is high in the air, dangling from the limb. These electrical wires are big boys—about three quarters of an inch thick. You get close to them and your hair kind of stands on end. Below the tree is nothing but rock wall. My dad goes out there with us. He tells us to cut down the treetop, and that's pretty much it. He has other jobs to attend to.

Okay...

I climb the tree and I am freezing my ass off. All of the weight of the treetop is on this one limb that could snap at any second. Normally I would try to position in above the limb to have a place to support my weight, then use a saw to take the limb down. But because the treetop has snapped off there is no up above. I tentatively step out onto the limb, wearing a safety harness. I can see that this is ridiculously dangerous. It reminds me of my dad yelling at me to *drop the damn ski*. I was scared but did not want to disappoint him.

However...

I'm thinking to myself that I have the possibility of excelling in the decathlon. I am convinced now that I have an affinity for it. I want to train for it, for the first time in my life push myself beyond what comes naturally. I've got other things to do besides stepping out onto a limb that might snap. I don't want to trim this tree. I don't particularly like trees. I really don't like climbing trees when it's Siberia outside in eastern Connecticut.

The saddle is attached to a rope, so it's easy for me to zip down. I go to my co-worker and tell him it's silly and I'm freezing to death and he should go do it. He looks at me like I'm crazy. So we go to the truck and turn the heater on and continue the discussion.

I ain't going up there.

I'm not going up there, either.

We are satisfied with our decision when all of a sudden my dad drives up. I roll the window down.

What are you guys doing?

Dad, I got up there. There's no safe place to cut the limb.

It's freezing cold, that branch could break off easily, and you have nothing but high-tension wires and rock wall below it. I don't like it. I'm not doing it.

The co-worker chimes in:

I ain't doing it either.

My dad looks at me:

Don't do this to me.

Dad, you're not going to convince me. This is a scary one, okay?

Don't do this to me.

Silence...

He grabs the rope that is still attached to the tree in his jacket and tie. He shimmies up with two hands as high as he can in his jacket and tie. He balances himself on the limb in his jacket and tie. He takes the saw and perfectly drops the pieces in between the electrical wires in his jacket and tie. He shimmies down the rope hand over hand in his jacket and tie. He doesn't say a word in his jacket and tie. He gets in his car and drives away in his jacket and tie.

I do think now about why my dad kept saying "don't do this to me." It may have been my defiance, which given past history was something he hated. Or the realization that I was never going to work in the tree business, not that that's what he had in mind. Maybe he thought I was cowardly. But I was also saying to my dad:

Please don't do this to me.

You have to let me live my life. Whatever it is and wherever it goes. I need to do something that totally preoccupies me, removes from my mind what is churning inside. I have never competed in a decathlon.

I may not be even good.

But I am going to try like hell.

—⚹—

Chapter Four

Who Am I?

I am looking in the mirror in a suite of the Queen Elizabeth Hotel in Montreal the morning after my Olympic win. I am naked with the gold medal around my neck. Now that it's over, who am I?

I am trying to see if I feel different after winning the gold and setting a world record and already being offered a broadcasting job by ABC.

The world's greatest athlete.

Nobody can say that except the thirteen gold medalists who have come before.

But I don't feel particularly different. I look into the mirror and I still see what I always see to one degree or another—a person who in working so hard to erase what is inside him has overcome nothing. Now that the Grand Diversion of training for the Olympics is over, now that I have won, what happens next? Will I find something else to preoccupy me, to take the edge off? My wife, Chrystie, is sleeping in the next room. She thinks she knows me almost four years into our marriage. She does know me.

She doesn't know me at all.

My fingers feel like talons, my shoulders and arms humped and ridged with bony muscles. My hair...I hate my hair no matter how long I try to make it. I look into my eyes. I take a few steps closer and burrow into them. What do I see?

What do you *see*?

I still see Bruce Jenner.

Not the Bruce Jenner the world now sees and wants and desires.

The Bruce Jenner I never wanted and never desired.

I am proud of my accomplishment. The day of the closing ceremonies at the Munich Olympics in 1972, where I finished tenth as a twenty-two-year-old, even I was surprised to have gotten that far. I wondered, *But what if I spend every minute of the next four years of my life training? What if I test myself to the limits to see how good I can become at something?*

I did exactly that.

But now that I have won, how special it could possibly be if I could do it. I am a skilled athlete who works harder than the rest, who has to prove his manhood more than the rest. I may act self-assured, but I still am not. I may exude an attractive confidence, but I feel neither confident nor attractive.

I still see Bruce Jenner.

*   *   *

I look in the mirror and think of Chrystie.

Her maiden name was Crownover. We met at the end of freshman year at Graceland. She was the daughter of a minister and, like me, lived a sheltered and cloistered life: my only sexual experience had been that one night my senior year in high school in the backseat of my mom's car. She was not aware of my gender issues when we started dating sophomore year, and I wasn't about to tell her, not then.

Chrystie was smart and assertive, the first in what would become a trend of wives who were also the same way. They took care of me, did everything for me, and I let them do everything for me, not simply because it made my life easier but because of my own internal weakness that only got worse over time. I am averse to confrontation; my only comeback is too often a whiny petulance. I felt I did not deserve to be assertive. I did not deserve to be proud. All of my marriages had a distinct pattern: compatibility and love followed by eventual unraveling.

Chrystie and I fell in love quickly. When we made love, it was warm and gentle, two people discovering our physicality. I also had my sights then set on the 1972 Olympics, a thought ridiculous to everyone except L.D. and Chrystie. That was when the Grand Diversion began to kick into gear, training every afternoon after classes from three to six p.m., only quitting so I could get to the cafeteria for dinner before it closed.

We moved in together, a huge step given the moral values of Graceland (the school had only a year earlier sponsored its first dance ever, girls on one side of the room and boys on the other and everyone terrified of the middle).

I didn't tell my parents. She did not tell her parents. We did not discuss marriage, except that I knew an athlete whose wife supported him so he could train, and I felt it was wrong to use his spouse like that. Chrystie disagreed, saying that if a husband and wife were working together toward a goal they both shared, then it did not matter who was supporting whom financially. Which is primarily why Chrystie went on to become a flight attendant for United Airlines.

At the end of December 1972, several months after the Munich Olympics, we got married. We were both in our early twenties, and I think we both had the same attitude that if you were going out into the big, bad world, it was a lot easier to do it with someone else. We had our wedding at the chapel at Graceland where I was finishing up my degree. There were about twenty guests, including my parents and her parents. Then we drove to Des Moines, where we had reserved a suite at the Holiday Inn, which for us was very swanky. The suite was not quite what we expected, since it actually had no bed. So we switched rooms and I carried Chrystie over the threshold, and by then it was ten p.m. We hadn't eaten dinner, so we tried to order room service but it was closed, and then we tried takeout, but every place had a two-hour wait. So we went to McDonald's for an intimate wedding night supper. We were planning to splurge on a trip to Hawaii, but then our car gave out and we spent pretty much all our money to fix it. But we still managed to spend a week there on two hundred dollars.

I told Chrystie in 1973 about my gender issues. It wasn't by choice: she was putting clothes away and noticed a rubber band on one of the hooks of her bra. When she asked me about it, my first response was noncommittal:

Gee, I don't know.

It was not very convincing. Rubber bands don't mysteriously appear on the hooks of bras. There was no way out.

That's why the rubber band, because I've been wearing your clothes.

She was totally shocked. She didn't know anyone who cross-dressed (neither did I) and had very little understanding of the whole thing (so did I). But she was overwhelmed with compassion and gratitude that I trusted her enough to tell her. Of course she was also relieved that I was not cross-dressing in front of her and never would. I tried to pass it off as just a phase, a fantasy that some men have, and hey, all men have fantasies anyway. Chrystie processed it as simply a piece of information, and then it was time for me to go back to being a guy.

We moved to San Jose so I could do nothing but train eight hours a day for the Montreal Olympics. We picked out an apartment roughly twenty yards from the San Jose City College track: all I had to do was climb over the fence and begin training. On a good day I could throw the discus into the middle of the field from our little third-floor balcony.

Together we formed a true marital partnership. Her powerful demeanor was an antidote to my soft one. She was the primary breadwinner while I fanatically trained, and she acted as buffer and protector, since it was my inclination to say yes to everything and Chrystie was the one who stepped in and said no. As the Olympics neared, the media became interested and began to play up the partnership angle. There were stories here and there, and then ABC's Roone Arledge amped it up.

The president of ABC Sports singlehandedly took the Olympics and transformed it from an event of minimal interest into a television sensation, the fee for rights going from $597,000 for the 1964 Winter Games to $25 million for the Montreal games. Arledge committed the network to an unprecedented 76.5 hours of coverage. He was the father of the overcoming-adversity narrative where the athlete defied all odds, cue-the-violin schmaltz poems, or what the network called "Up Close and Personal." He saw them as potentially enormous rating boosters, and in particular he saw Chrystie and me as the stars of the show.

I would not be at the Olympics without Chrystie. I would not be staring into the mirror with a gold medal around my neck. But I also wonder if now that the Grand

Diversion is over, will the woman living inside me still be content to remain quiet, or will she want more? And if that happens, if my gender issues only heighten, what will happen to Chrystie and me?

I look in the mirror and there is something dreamlike about it all. Bruce did it. He actually did it. He beat the defending champion, Mykola Avilov of the Soviet Union. It was more than simply defeating Avilov. It was beating the Red Menace of the Soviet Union at the peak of the Cold War. Roughly a year and a half earlier, in April 1975, South Vietnam had fallen to communist forces. The Soviets were intent on spreading their domination by military force, such as the invasion of Afghanistan three and a half years later.

The Olympics had become more of a test of nationalist prowess and strength than ever before. The medal count had never been more important, the barometer by which countries were considered strong or weak.

The Soviets were on their way to winning forty-nine gold medals, East Germany forty, and the United States thirty-four. The overall performance was a terrible disappointment, particularly in track where the American men's and women's teams netted one individual gold medal. The days in Montreal were winding down, and the only major events left were the finals in men's basketball and the decathlon. I was the overwhelming favorite to win. At the 1976 US Olympic Trials in Eugene I set a world record.

I have lost one decathlon in three years, because I was bored, and losing was actually good because it renewed my commitment.

Because of all the disappointment in the US team, it was falling on me to salvage the country's performance. It wasn't only that we needed to defeat the Soviets. Our country was convulsing in the aftermath of Watergate, the resignation of Richard Nixon as president, and the debacle of Vietnam. Our political system had failed us. Our once-sacred values had failed us. We felt weak and confused. We were a country adrift. Sports could help right us. It was that powerful. Just to make the pressure a little bit more intense, the country had celebrated its bicentennial just a few weeks earlier. Patriotism was at its peak. Heroes were at a premium.

But it got to me when I watched teammate Dave Roberts, the overwhelming favorite in the pole vault, lose because of heavy rain. The rain? How could I control the weather when the decathlon started three days later?

Oh, Chrystie, I've got to carry the whole United States...

My knees buckled. My body felt fragile, crushed. For the first time I wondered if I could handle the pressure. I started crying as Chrystie held me. She tried to encourage me. Then we both realized the same thing: It rains, it rains. It snows, it snows. It hails, it hails. The ground collapses beneath us, the ground collapses beneath us.

There was not a thing I could do about any of it except go out and do it.

As usual the waiting for the damn thing to begin was excruciating. I entered the stadium and psyched myself up and worked out a little bit until I realized that no amount of working out was going to help at this moment. Either you have trained enough or you haven't. Either you embrace the pressure or you choke. But I still had to wait for endless inspections by the International Olympic Committee: length of spikes, height of soles for the shoe used in the long jump, making sure the number I had been assigned matched the master set. It only made it harder to maintain focus.

I watched the first heat of the 100 meters on a closed-circuit television. Avilov with his drooping moustache was in the first heat. I hoped it would slow him down. I would have shaved the damn thing off.

False start.

False start.

False start.

This was good, very good.

Somebody was overanxious.

The fourth start was clean. Avilov, responsible for one of the false starts, was slow and lumbering off the mark. He was a step behind after ten meters and only lagging farther behind. He finished in 11.23 seconds, significantly worse than his Munich time of 11.00. Decathlons are measured by personal bests, and Avilov hasn't come close.

The second heat...

I ran 10.94 seconds, the best 100 meters I had ever run in my life under the conditions, seventy points more than Avilov.

I had him. I knew I had him with nine events still to go. His concentration was off. Mine was like a tight wire. So that was when I knew I was going to win, the lever of momentum fast and furious, the golden moment of omnipotence that the athlete feels when he can race to the moon and be back in time for dinner with a side trip to the sun.

I look in the mirror and think about what I did after I actually won.

A spectator ran out from the stands and handed me a small American flag. I was surprised by the gesture. I wanted to run a victory lap, and I had the flag of my country with me, and I was not going to hand it to someone else to hold or put it down, because that would be disrespectful, so I circled the track with it. Legend has it that I was the first American Olympic champion in history to take a victory lap waving the flag. But that image, unplanned and so tiny in the course of a life, is what defines me, what people remember most. The flag was an extension of me, the patriotism and pride I felt as I circled the track becoming patriotism and pride all Americans could feel. We all just won.

* * *

I look in the mirror and I can still see the tears in the eyes of my parents when I find them in the stands. But in the eyes of my mom, as sincere as my dad sometimes is not, I didn't see euphoria but a split-second of fear.

Fear that fame would change me no matter how much I resist it. Fear that I would become addicted to fame no matter how much I resist it. Fear that my ability to make emotional connections and reach out—already tenuous—would completely disappear as I am swallowed up into the public. Fear that the attention, no matter how much I tried to reject it, would become an addiction.

I might be imagining it. But hearing my mother many years later, maybe I'm not:

> When it was finally decided that he was going to Graceland, I kind of figured he'd wind up to be a coach, a college coach, probably track. And do you know something, I sometimes wished that had happened.
>
> Fame and fortune takes the family apart. And I thought, you know, if he had come in second in Montreal, no one would know his name and wouldn't it be wonderful if he had just had a much more normal life, got married, had his kids and a closer relationship.

When our kids are growing up we wish for them to have fame and fortune and be successful, and we think of it monetarily mostly, that that brings happiness. But I think in my head now, "be careful what you wish for because you might just get it."

I don't wonder about that now when I look in the mirror with that medal around my neck. All of that is yet to come.

I only know that I am naked and about to become an American hero.

—⚬—

October 14, 2015

"Breast forms…"

I am on the phone with my stepdaughter Kim.

She asks me what I am up to. I tell her I am about to go through the downstairs closet of my Malibu home to get rid of what Bruce used to wear. She says to wait and will be right over. I am not entirely sure why, although I don't think it is because she needs more clothing.

She arrives. She wants to save several items for herself and her sisters as a way to remember who I once was, almost as if there has been a death in the family. It is mostly everyday stuff I used to wear, plus the suits I donned when I gave speeches. It is the same thing she did when her father Robert died, carting away several bags of his clothing to forever honor his memory.

I don't know what she will ultimately do with them, keep them tucked away in a remote corner somewhere or probably forget about them, as is the fate of most keepsakes.

Getting rid of the clothing has been much harder than I thought. It was not nearly as exhilarating or exciting as

I initially thought it would be, that feeling that *this is so great, I can finally get rid of what Bruce wore since I don't need them anymore.* Instead there has been an undeniable feeling of loss even for me. So maybe there has been a death in the family.

It is interesting to me the degree to which writers and commentators on transgender issues speak on my behalf and tell readers what I am thinking or feeling without ever talking to me. Right after I transitioned, Meredith Ramirez Talusan wrote on Fusion.net that Bruce was a so-called "dead name" and should never be used again. "It's a matter of basic courtesy," wrote Talusan. "Jenner hasn't just definitively announced her true gender, but also let go of a male identity that she's felt alienated from since early childhood. If she thinks of her life in her male role as a lie, then it's also true that her former name, the one that stands in for that life, is also a lie."

Bruce was not a lie. Bruce existed: what I did lie about or at least obfuscate was Caitlyn's existence. Talusan suggested that the headline should have been TRANSGENDER OLYMPIC CHAMPION ANNOUNCES HER NAME: CAITLYN, which is not only a very big mouthful but untrue since I was not a transgender Olympic champion at that time but Bruce Jenner. If I were a transgender woman, I would have been stripped of the medal for competing in a men's event.

Bruce won the Olympics. I lived as a man before I transitioned. I had a life as Bruce, and the more comfortable

I become as Caitlyn, the more I actually embrace Bruce as a valuable part of my life. I obviously don't want to be called Bruce, but I am not going to bury him and send him to the "dead name" pile. There has to be some reality here, at least for me. You can't simply blot out your past, your beliefs, your interests. The life that you lived as a father and dad and husband, the accomplishments and failures, do not get sent to the trash with a click of the mouse.

I remember crying when I received my new birth certificate from the state of New York stating that I am female and giving my name as Caitlyn Marie Jenner. They were tears of joy in seeing the correct gender marker on such an important legal document. But there were also tears of sadness that Bruce was gone, the birth certificate being official proof.

After the Diane Sawyer interview on ABC and the subsequent *Vanity Fair* cover and story, I got a letter from a trans woman named Jody who lives in Los Angeles. She transitioned fifteen years ago. Jody told me perhaps the most instructive story I have heard from a trans person. The subject of gender came up. Jody said it was three or four years after her transition when she put her head to the pillow one night. It was a night like any other except for something momentous: she had gone the whole day without thinking about gender.

I have not reached that point. I don't want to give the impression that I am thinking, *Is this really me?* But I do think about gender. I am firmly on the side of womanhood now. But I am not a woman. Nor will I ever be.

I am a trans woman. There is a difference.

I never menstruated or had menopause. I obviously cannot give birth. I was never screwed out of a job because of the sexism that is still pervasive.

Is my gender female? Yes. Has it always been female? Yes. I use the women's restroom because I am a woman. I changed the gender on my birth certificate to female because I am a woman. But it's a different kind of womanhood for me. And that will never change. I'm fine with that. It doesn't diminish Caitlyn.

I'm glad when Kim carts off several bags of clothing to her car. I need the closet space. Plus the best stuff, all the athletic gear I wore over the years as Bruce, I'm still keeping.

I never told her about the drawer full of breast forms and hip pads I used to wear. They are in the bedroom closet where all of Caitlyn's clothes now hang. I don't need any of them now, so I wonder why I even kept them. But then I realized why: they symbolize my struggle when I was Bruce, but they are also part of the journey of my life. I can't ignore them. I don't want to ignore them.

I pack them up into a box. I know exactly where I am going to put them: in the garage next to the accordion.

—◇—

Chapter Five

Golden Boy

It doesn't even take a day before the sportswriters, intent on finding a story to take out of the Olympics, start furiously tapping their typewriter keys. They need a happy ending. America needs a happy ending. The aura of male invincibility they ascribe to me is already in high gear: I am an athlete who comes along once in a millennium, or so they write.

> Bruce Jenner's next move should be the rental of a Brinks truck. Prince Valiant with muscles...Imagine. A movie. Our hero is handsome beyond right. His wife is a beautiful blonde who wears a yellow t-shirt with the words "Go Jenner Go" on the back. Our hero is winning the decathlon, the event that from Jim Thorpe's day has been the measure of the world's greatest athlete.
>
> —DAVID KINDRED,
> THE COURIER-JOURNAL OF LOUISVILLE

Bruce Jenner, the golden boy from San Jose, Calif.

—ROBERT FACHET, *WASHINGTON POST*

Bruce Jenner of San Jose, Calif., wants to be a movie or television star. After his record-breaking victory in the Olympic decathlon today, he probably can be anything he wants.

—FRANK LITSKY, *THE NEW YORK TIMES*

Hollywood-handsome.

—ASSOCIATED PRESS

Bruce Jenner always says the right thing at the right time, no matter what the place...everything that glitters is Bruce Jenner.

—PHIL HERSH, *CHICAGO DAILY NEWS*

This is a couple America will not be allowed to forget...

—KENNETH DENLINGER, *THE WASHINGTON POST*

Jenner is twirling the nation like a baton; he and his wife, Chrystie, are so high up on the pedestal of American heroism, it would take a crane to get them down.

—TONY KORNHEISER,
NEW YORK TIMES

The only thing missing is that I have this woman living inside me. I don't like what I see when I dress up: big arms, legs long but too muscular, no clothes that really fit. It is all great for the decathlon but not very good for a night out on the town. But the last thing I can do is physically alter my appearance in any way. The sportswriters won't tolerate it. America won't tolerate it.

I will continue to play the game of Bruce, the demands upon him never greater. That's actually good, a new zone of preoccupation. But being busy is only a distraction, not a solution.

Otherwise the sportswriters nailed it.

I am not innocent in all the hoopla. I know I am photogenic and telegenic and wholesome, actually because I am photogenic and telegenic and wholesome, and so is my wife. Our partnership is a legitimate story, and the media laps it up. We play along with it even though we are beginning to have problems. We do interviews together and appearances together and present ourselves as the ultimate apple-pie couple.

A few in the media suggest that I had a game plan in place before the Olympics on how to capitalize if I won. Did I hope there would be opportunities? Of course. Remember, these were the days of true amateurism, when there were no financial sponsorships. But I had no idea what they would be nor did I care. I only wanted to win. Chrystie only wanted to win. If I had never gotten a single endorsement after the Games, that would have been fine.

Now there are opportunities. Some are beyond silly—General Mills actually wanted me to jump out of an over-sized Wheaties box for the sake of some cheap promotion. But I do intuitively understand the media game and the fame game and the endorsement game. It is all a game and you have to play it. I am all too aware of what happened to Mark Spitz, the American swimmer who won seven gold medals at the 1972 games and set seven world records in every event in which he participated. The hope was that Spitz would become the first American Olympian to parlay his performance into a fortune. It was projected that Spitz might get $5 million in endorsements, and there were hyperbolic predictions of a major film career. But, to me, he just didn't have the personality for the camera. He scored a legendary bomb on a Bob Hope special two months after the Games and, in my estimation, quickly proved to the film industry that not only could he not act but he didn't like acting.

I also believe he burned a lot of bridges with companies he endorsed. He never seemed very good at the shadow dance with either the media or sponsors, which entails being endlessly deferential and appreciative. I once heard him say he spent fifteen years on his swimming and fifteen minutes on his speeches. It just didn't seem like he was cut out for this kind of life.

I try not to make the same mistakes as Spitz. Already at this point in my life I know I am a good actor even if I have never appeared in a single thing. If I have successfully hidden my true self from the world, how hard can it be to do film or television? At least I know I can cross-dress.

I prove it when I do a Bob Hope special on NBC after the Games. I appear with Bob and former Los Angeles Rams defensive lineman–turned–actor Merlin Olsen as the "Melody Maids." The gag is that we are going to appear with Bob in drag together, which for me isn't a gag but something of a godsend. I have to be careful not to show too much enthusiasm, so I play it cool, guy's guys dressing up like a woman. *Yuk-yuk-yuk.*

Bob looks the best of the three of us. Merlin's beard is not working for him. Our wigs and dresses are purposely ridiculous. But the red heels I think not only look good on me but also fit, so I steal them after the show.

Forty years later I am ready to return them.

It is a tremendous high to go out and conquer the world physically. I feel like a gladiator going into the arena and being the only one left standing. I don't want to diminish that. But the Games have only made me feel strong physically. They don't make me feel strong emotionally. I don't feel like I remotely have my act together, a place in life that truly fits. I still feel weak. I still feel unworthy.

But suck it up, Little Brucie. Suck it up. Play the game.

You've always been good at games.

So work it, little Brucie. Work it.

And by the way, tell the woman inside you to keep her mouth shut.

In the aftermath of Montreal I become a staple of

the talk show circuit, often appearing with Chrystie: *Good Morning America* with David Hartman as host and Billy Carter as guest; the *Tonight Show with Johnny Carson* and guests John Davidson (remember), Madlyn Rhue (don't remember), and Steven Landesberg (*Barney Miller*, right?); a weeklong stint on *The Mike Douglas Show* with Chrystie as co-host; *Dinah!* opposite a repeat of *Marcus Welby, M.D.*, *The Edge of Night*, and *The Bugs Bunny Show*.

I have my portrait taken by the world-renowned photographer Francesco Scavullo for a book he is working on and spontaneously do a handstand. I am mobbed on the streets of New York for autographs, surrounded by a chain of whispers of "There's Bruce Jenner!" at every major airport in America. I talk to everyone. But the talk is small and getting smaller; like Chrystie, I wonder how much is left for me after the exhaustion of being besieged.

My business manager, George Wallach, is not making it any easier to have a few quiet days off. He says in print that I have as much film potential as Robert Redford and that my reception in New York was similar to that after Charles Lindbergh had completed his historic nonstop flight to Paris. I have rejected several endorsements offered immediately after the Games as well as other business opportunities. I want to be in this for the long run and not look like a money whore, but George's public boasting is running the risk of the same oversaturation as Spitz. I need to take it slow.

But it's hard to keep your head straight when soon after the Games the producers of the film *Superman* want me to test for the title role. It's a little bit of a stretch—actually, it's absurd. I have never done a screen test in my life. "I'll have to see the script, though I think I can identify with the part," I quip. I like new challenges, and I am hoping to act someday, so Chrystie and I fly to Rome. They have me do a fight scene with a stand-in playing the evil villain Lex Luthor. Then they feed me lines. They tell me I'm "great," and I think they mean it.

But there is an immediate problem.

They want me to cut my hair for the role, and I won't do it. My hair is one of the few ways I can feel my femininity, and it is these tentacles that keep me going, make me feel some tiny piece of my authentic self.

After not hearing from the producers for roughly a year, I learn the role is given to Christopher Reeve—and at that point I don't particularly care whether I will be cast or not. Not caring—another familiar motif in my life after the Games.

I am living the dream, and sometimes it feels like a dream, or at least enough of a diversion to suppress my gender issues. I miss the Grand Diversion terribly, that feeling of waking up every day and knowing exactly what I was going to do. I don't know how I am going to replace it, although I have given it considerable thought.

I knew I wanted out of sports, which is why I left my vaulting pole in the Olympic stadium. It's always better to finish an athletic career at the top instead of being shoved out at the bottom when it's obvious to everyone except to the athlete that the skill is gone. I don't want to get caught in the trap of not preparing for when your career is finished. I have seen it too many times and witnessed the devastation too many times. You stay terrified of doing something different. You are coddled for so much of your life that you have no clue how to live on your own. Plus, let's be honest: there isn't much demand for a decathlete outside of the Games. It takes two days, there are ten events, and anybody who says they truly understand the scoring is lying. I want to leverage my athletic success if I can, not depend on it.

I officially sign with ABC in October 1976, where I will ultimately become a jack-of-all-trades and master of none. I like learning the new skill of broadcasting and being on air. But I don't lock on to it. There is no mission to be the best. I have lost my ultracompetitive instinct, odd for someone who had such a strong one.

As much as I loved the Grand Diversion, I have concluded that it can be dangerous to become so obsessed with competitiveness and winning. It stunts you from ever growing as a person: all you are on Earth for is to train, score points, win. Nothing else mattered for me when I was determined to win the decathlon in Montreal, which I know was a tremendous source of frustration for Chrystie and my parents. When I was with them, I wasn't present in the moment but far off in my own moment—faster, higher, stronger. As much as I loved the single-mindedness of that, I never want to be that single-minded again. And yet I need to be single-minded in something if I am to keep my gender issues in check, so it is a difficult contradiction.

I am single-minded so I can live. I am not single-minded so I can live. Caught once again in the middle.

I see right away my limitations in broadcasting, the demon of dyslexia still intent on humiliating me, the past always prologue. ABC wants to try me out as the permanent co-host of *Wide World of Sports* with Frank Gifford in Los Angeles and myself in New York. We do a practice run, and it is clear I cannot handle the teleprompter because I am a slow reader. The words scroll through the monitor too quickly. I cannot keep pace.

I try to get over the hurdle of the teleprompter. I learn to memorize the script and make progress. But from the very beginning I am marginalized.

My first assignment is on a show called *Battle of the Network Stars* as an on-field reporter offering commentary and asking contestants how they feel after they do running and swim relays and 100-yard dashes and tugs-of-war and hitting a golf ball with accuracy. The show debuts on November 13, 1976; it is wacky and kind of oddly wonderful, a celebrity Olympics with animated fireworks at the beginning in which the participants show up in limos. There is no teleprompter to work with, which is good. I do well given my inexperience. People respond positively to my friendly and casual style. I feel good about myself, and when that happens, my gender issues go into semi-hibernation. I feel as close to a sense of peace as I can get.

For exactly seventeen days after the show's debut.

*   *   *

My brother Burt and I have never been particularly close for much of our lives. He is eight years younger, for one thing. He also has the misfortune of living in the shadow and footsteps of my exploits. He is a very good athlete himself. But he is tired of the endless comparisons in football and basketball and track. My mom remembers it best:

> It was difficult for Burt and I blame these damn teachers and coaches, Burt being so much younger than Bruce and Bruce already in high school and the star. Coaches would come down the hall and run into Burt and say "Hey, young Jenner, we're waiting for you!" What a lot of pressure was on that little boy that he has to live up to when he hasn't had a chance to get started.
>
> He was a very good athlete but he would not compete in anything that Bruce did. He wouldn't compete in it. He was the fastest on the track in intramurals but he wouldn't go out for track. And the coaches wanted him to and pressured him to, but he wouldn't budge. He was built just like Bruce. Actually I think he was better looking, too.

Burt reacts by doing the opposite of everything I did. I played football. He plays soccer. I waterskied. He snow skis. I was a mediocre student. He is a very good student.

I am frustrated that he shies away from certain competitive sports, because I know how good he can be. There is tension between us, and the emotional distance only intensifies after I leave for Graceland at eighteen when he is ten. We both share vivid memories of the one and only time in my life I got drunk as a senior in high school and slept with him in the same bed because I could not make it to the top bunk. He was mad at me, and I was mad at him for not moving to the top bunk when I asked. From then on I only see him when I come home.

About nine months before the Montreal Games our relationship improves. I am more mature and he is about to graduate from high school, and he asks to talk to me privately one day, telling me that he wants to come to California, if Chrystie and I end up there permanently after the Games, and live with us. His plan is to work for a year to establish residency and then apply to an in-state school at virtually no cost. I like the idea. I like it because it will be a way of drawing us closer.

He is there in Montreal with my parents, Chrystie, and about sixty friends and family. Recently I saw the picture in *Sports Illustrated* that was taken of the entourage after I won. They were easy to pick out since they were all wearing those yellow T-shirts with GO JENNER GO on the back, very proud canaries. I could pick out everyone in the picture, except for Burt. He wasn't there. I could not find him. Where was he? Why wasn't he there? Where had he gone?

* * *

Burt's bags are all packed on November 30, 1976. They are neatly side by side in his room like standing soldiers, ready to go. I am in town to do a speaking engagement in Canton, Connecticut, where he is living with my parents. We have tickets for an afternoon flight to Los Angeles out of Hartford. Chrystie and I have just bought a house in Malibu, and Burt is going to live on the first floor.

Because I am going to be in Canton for several days, a local car dealer, knowing my weakness for Porsches, drops off a 911 model so I can have a car to drive.

I let Burt use it a little bit. For an eighteen-year-old kid who has just graduated from high school, few things in life, if anything, are sweeter than tooling around town in a Porsche 911. Burt is also responsible.

He won't do anything stupid.

The speech is at nine a.m. We are leaving for the airport several hours later, so Burt says he can take care of filling the car with gas so the tank will be full when it is returned to the dealer.

The service station is only about a mile away, and on the route is Canton High School. Burt cannot resist driving in front of the entrance. He sees a girl he knows that is a good friend.

Hey, jump in. We'll go down and get some gas, and I'll bring you right back.

Her name is Judith Hutchings, and she is sixteen. She

hops in and off they go down a back road that he has driven hundreds of times.

I am wrapping up my speech. My dad is in the audience listening. He cannot see the back of the room. But I can, and it seems strange when three policemen walk in. They ask if they can speak to us privately and then take us into a classroom. We still don't know what is going on until one of them says:

There's been a serious accident involving your son. You should get to the hospital right away.

I drive. My dad is next to me. He is banging on the dashboard as hard as he can, and I think he is going to break his hand. I remember him saying:

Goddammit! Goddammit! This is going to kill your mother!

Burt has a special place in my mother's soul. She pleaded with Bill to have another child when he thought two was enough. There is a tenderness to Burt that steals her heart, a sweet and gentle softness I never possessed as her oldest son. He does what he is told. He does not argue. He even takes calculus.

My mom is at home when the phone rings. It is the police. They tell her that one of her sons has been in an accident and has been transported to the hospital. They never give a name, so she does not know whether it's Burt or me. She comes out of the apartment pale and shaking. A next-door neighbor, a young mother, sees her and asks what happened, and she tells her there has been an accident involving one of her sons. The young mother can tell she is terrified.

You're not driving.

She takes my mom to the nearest hospital in Farmington. She learns that it is Burt who is injured. But he isn't there. He has been taken to a larger hospital in Hartford.

They don't mention to her that it's a trauma center.

Burt had taken the Porsche on Old Canton Road. Because the road was old, it was also narrow and curvy. There was a rise, and Burt took it too fast. The Porsche went airborne and then crooked. It hit a tree and then a rock wall of sizable boulders. Hutchings was flung from the car and killed instantly. Burt suffered critical injuries.

My dad is typically stoic as we drive, with his residual toughness. He says little, if anything. He had seen so much horror in the war, I wonder if that is what he is thinking now and maybe trying to brace himself for whatever happened. Although I also know that whatever he saw, it never involved his son, his flesh and blood.

My mom is already there in a waiting room when we arrive. They try to give her tranquilizers but she refuses, because there is no way she is going to put up with that.

One of the neurosurgeons comes in. My mom remembers it vividly:

You get to the hospital and a surgeon comes down and talks to you and says "I hate to tell you this but your son cannot live." Oh God. And then you sit around for hours as Bill and I talk and the doctors say "we have him on life support. We can keep his heart going and his breathing going for who knows how long because he's so young and so strong, but there are no brain waves." Bill and I talk it over for a few hours and go back and forth into his room. He was lying there, they had him all cleaned up and the damage was to the back of his head so you can't see it and he's lying on the bed and you say to yourself "My God there's nothing wrong with him! He can't be dying."

Dad and Mom make their decision.
We want him taken off life support.
My mom puts her cheek on her youngest son's cheek before he dies. She whispers to him for the final time:
I love you wherever you are now.
It's just like my mom described. He still looks beautiful when the machines are dismantled. He still looks just like Burt, the eighteen-year-old kid who has figured out the next step of his life. The Burt I am just getting to know. The Burt who in his yearbook, which I found and looked at the day after he died, used a lyric from Cat Stevens's "Peace Train" as his favorite words of inspiration:

*Now I've been smiling lately, thinking about the good
    things to come
And I believe it could be, something good has begun*

That same day my dad and I go to the funeral home

to pick out a casket. I have never been to a funeral home before. I have never picked out a casket before.

But now I am, for my brother.

I have struggled with the issue of guilt. What if I had never taken the car from the dealer? What if I had never lent it to Burt? Why did he pick up an innocent young woman who had her whole life in front of her? Why did he drive so carelessly? But never in my life have I ever beat myself up about it. It is a mechanism of protection, I know, but I have come to the conclusion that it was Burt's day to die, just as, on the beaches of Normandy, it was my father's day not to. It was the way it was. That's what happened. The accident had a fate and will of its own: two people tragically lost their lives, and my brother was the one responsible. But I have to move on because so much of my life has been about moving on—get over it, get through it, don't show outward emotion because it only leads to inner emotions, and I must keep those in check. The floodgates open and I am done. It is why I could not bear to view the casket and not wait to leave town when the funeral was over.

For many months after his passing my mom could not bear to go inside his room, so it remained the way it was, with those bags packed and ready to go like standing soldiers, for an afternoon flight to California he never got to take and never will.

—m—

Chapter Six

What Goes Up . . .

I am waiting for it.

No story lasts forever, and the one of God and country and Bruce going out and winning the Games and becoming the golden boy and Prince Valiant and the hero and the face of the Wheaties box and having a lovely flight attendant wife who steadfastly supported him through thick and thin is too good to last forever. The media loves you until they hate you. They elevate, then denigrate. They fixate, then grow bored. They make you larger than life, then smaller than life. Anybody in the public eye knows that. The guillotine of celebrity. Try to prolong your reign for as long as possible before they take your head.

I just don't want to make it easier for them. But in the late 1970s and early 1980s there is ammunition if they can locate the cache. There are whispers of Bruce the playboy and Bruce the asshole. So I am waiting. But you are still not prepared for it. The only solace is that after six months the media will move on to something else. (Remember, this is pre-Internet. The attention span of the media now is more like six minutes, but it only takes six minutes for a story to go around the world and back.)

I knew this going in. No one can sustain the qualities ascribed to me, the hyper hyperbole. I have tried to live an exemplary life, but no one lives a totally exemplary one. I still believe every word of the "Finding the Champion Within" speech, how you don't have to be great at any-thing to be great, how single-mindedness and hard work and a fixed goal can take you to wherever you want to go. The panties and the bra underneath is my little bonus.

But Chrystie and I are fraying: we are not a perfect partnership because there is no perfect partnership. Train-ing for the Olympics was simple; we had no needs and very little money. We lived in an apartment that cost $145 a month. Nobody knew who we were. It was so easy and innocent compared to the pressures of trying to live up to something you know you are not. It's extraordinarily dif-ficult under any circumstances. But for me...

Sometimes I wonder if it would be better to run away, just disappear. But where?

In 1978 Chrystie and I have our first child, Burt, named after my brother. He is a beautiful baby and will turn out to be a beautiful son: tough, fiercely independent, loyal, the owner of a burgeoning dog-sitting business that he started from scratch.

It is a sublime moment, but only a moment. Chrystie thinks I am remote and frustrated, which I am. I find her snappish and angry over things that to me seem incidental. I feel hurt and she feels hurt. I sometimes worry that so much of my life is in the public eye now that there is nothing left of me in private, addicted to celebrity because it is your life, depleted by celebrity because it is your life, loving celebrity because it is your life, hating celebrity because it is your life.

My gender issues are there—gender issues are always there—but Chrystie and I have just grown apart. Those simple days were the best days. I don't believe I have changed since the Games: it is the entire world that has changed around me, literally overnight, a space capsule dropped into the ocean and a million people wanting to be the first to reach it and touch it and take home a tiny piece of it.

Chrystie leaves without telling me first. I come home and she is gone and so is our child and some of Chrystie's clothing. I don't know where she has gone, although I assume—correctly, as it turned out—that she is with her mother. Maybe she has grown weary of being in my shadow; maybe she feels I had become one-dimensional. Her recollection is that I had gotten bored and no longer cared about the marriage. I have my truth. She has hers. Anyone who has been in a serious relationship that is fighting for its life knows that both interpretations are likely correct.

We remain separated for several months. We are trying, but as in any wounded marriage, trying is often not enough. I am confused, bored, lonely. I need to try something totally out of my wheelhouse, at least take advantage of the Bruce Jenner reputation.

Enter Hugh Hefner.

The founder of Playboy Enterprises had invited Chrystie and me to his mansion in Los Angeles for his Thursday night at the movies in the past. We never went. But now that we are separated, the mansion does intrigue me.

There is no better way to make people think you are a testosterone-juiced male than hanging out at the mansion. It's not that I suddenly feel like a man's man. I actually have great difficulty making friends with men. I gravitate toward women because I far more readily identify with them and feel more comfortable with them, to the degree I feel comfortable with anyone. They are more fun, more feeling, more interesting. I feel I have more in common with them—I obviously do at this point—but women themselves only see the male athlete stereotype when they see me. The idea of us having something in common seems preposterous, so the conversations are often short and awkward. I can't let too much leak out anyway. Asking questions about eyebrow-plucking is a dead giveaway.

I am wary of overdoing it with women because I am always wary. So I laugh it up with the guys. It has been roughly three years since the Olympics and I am more entrenched in the role of Bruce than ever as I near thirty. At this point I have not only the Wheaties deal but other major endorsements as well including Minolta cameras and Tropicana. I also have my broadcasting career, and I am still curious about acting and getting genuine feelers.

My entire livelihood won't simply be jeopardized if I explore what is inside me; it will end. It is my nightmare, and it will be a recurring one as I weigh what to do. I just can't throw my career away. So I make a conscious choice that I am going to date women now, given the separation. I am also physically attracted to them. I need to make the point once again (and no doubt will again so it really sinks in) that your gender has nothing to do with your sexual preference. I also have a tendency, when I start to seriously date a woman, to end up marrying them.

I am a prude.

On May 1, 1979, I am at the Playboy Mansion for a charity tennis tournament for the John Tracy Clinic for people with hearing loss. The 22,000-square-foot home in Holmby Hills has twenty-nine rooms and a pool and a zoo and the infamous grotto lit up at night by sheets of purple and gold and green—a little bit like an open-air strip club, I would imagine (at this point in my life I have never been to a strip club).

I win the tournament. A woman named Linda Thompson gives out the winning trophy and a T-shirt. At the time she is twenty-eight years old and has a role on the television show *Hee Haw*, although her real claim to fame is having been Elvis Presley's girlfriend for four years (Presley died in August 1977, eight months after they broke up). I don't know any of this about Linda. Pop culture is a mystery to me (not so anymore): when my publicist asks at some point if I want to appear on Howard Stern's radio show, my first response is "Who the hell is Howard Stern?" because I have no idea.

I just know that we hit it off, and I find Linda fun and sexy and Southern-belle sweet. I am determined to ask her out, so I spend much of the night at the mansion, still in my sweaty tennis clothes, within an arm's length of her, outlasting the advances of George Peppard (who would later become the cigar-chomping leader on the television show *The A-Team*) until he finally gives up and leaves.

We begin to go out together. Nothing serious. We like to dance, shades of my mom and dad cutting it up with the Lindy on those forties dance floors. She knows I am separated because I tell her right away.

What are the odds of your getting back with your wife?

Fifty-fifty.

Then I'll be your friend, but I'm not going to be involved with you.

We continue to do things together. Chrystie hears about it and understandably brings up the subject. I tell her I have met someone I like. It is an obviously difficult moment. We are separated but still married. We have been through the lean years and the fat years and have built up a shared history I have never come close to having with anyone else. We have a baby we both love. Chrystie has been living in a rented beach house, and we decide we must try to reconcile. I call Linda and tell her I cannot see her anymore. Her hope is genuine that the marriage will work out. She sends me books on how to stay married.

I should have read them more closely.

There is a renewed physical intimacy between Chrystie and me when we come back together. I am twenty-nine now, and I find it lovely. We are both committed. All we have to do is look across the kitchen and see Burt in his high chair to know we have a responsibility to do everything we can to make it work. It is one of those urgent moments where I convince myself I can suppress my gender issues for good. If I can just cross-dress every now and then, I will be fine. I can manage. I can even be happy. Chrystie already knows I like to wear her bras.

We are together for three months. There are issues, but to me at least the renewed intimacy is a good sign. Then Chrystie moves out for a second time without telling me, back to San Jose to live with her mom. I come home one day from a speech on the road and she is gone, the bedroom closets empty. There is no note or explanation as far as I remember.

At this point the marriage is truly over.

If I can pinpoint a period in my life where the edges begin to disintegrate, it starts here with the end of my first marriage. The sequence of events is admittedly blurred. All of this is from my perspective, and no matter how much I search my soul it will always be from my perspective. I also know I did things I very much regret.

A month or two after Chrystie moves out for the second time, I get back in touch with Linda. Our relationship becomes serious. When you are supposed to be squeaky-clean Bruce Jenner and you are now hanging out at the Playboy Mansion and that's where you first met the last girlfriend of Elvis Presley and then you start dating her, there is no way to keep that private even though it is private. Stories leak out—ADONIS DUMPS WIFE FOR ELVIS-EX PRINCESS—or something like that.

Every storm passes. I believe that. Then Chrystie calls and tells me that she's pregnant. The news stuns me. It is not something we ever discussed, although when you do not use birth control, which we did not, you take the chance.

I suggest to her that given we are headed for divorce, she doesn't have to give birth and can get an abortion. I am thinking about what life will be like for a child brought into the world in which the parents are in divorce proceedings. And yes, I am thinking about my image and future livelihood.

Chrystie becomes livid. She makes it clear that the child is hers, not ours, and wants me to have nothing to do with raising the child. I bring up the issue of financial responsibility and ask why I should help support a child when the mother has told me to stay away. Maybe it sounds callous to anyone who has not been involved in a divorce. Nothing is ever framed the way it should be. You are blinded by emotion and view everything only from your own perspective.

With our marriage headed for divorce, I am not

prepared to have another child. I cannot emotionally handle another child. The idea of raising Burt as a divorced couple is hard enough.

All of this is intensely private and painful. But I am a public figure, which also means you have no private life. I am Mr. Squeaky Clean, and now I am dirty. At least that is how the media will portray it. I can see the story now, a new and juicier version—BRUCE JENNER LEAVES PREGNANT WIFE FOR ELVIS EX. The only good thing is that my comment about abortion will always remain private.

Linda and I continue to date. Chrystie moves back into the home we own in Malibu—I come home one day and all my stuff is in the garage. I move into a rented house on Las Flores Beach in Malibu. It's junky and small, but all of this is temporary.

I *will* outlast the media. Maybe it is better that I am not Bruce the golden boy. I can be seen as human now, far more real, although of course I am not close to real.

Chrystie gives birth on June 10, 1980. I am on the road in a hotel room in Kansas City when her mother calls to tell me that Cassandra was just born. I cry my eyes out, guilt-ridden over not being there, knowing that I should be there but also knowing that Chrystie did not want me there. I had always considered myself a person of high moral standing. I had always tried to do things right. But all of this has turned out so horribly wrong.

At least it can't get any more complicated...

Linda and I are at the Las Flores Beach house several

months later in the fall of 1980. She gives me a card that says "Congratulations" on the top. I am a little confused— I am not sure what I am to be congratulated about—until Linda tells me she is pregnant. I can envision the newest set of headlines: PRINCE VALIANT SWINGS MIGHTY SWORD MANY TIMES.

I tell her we must get married. I cannot bear any more hurt and pain in my life or anyone else's. I want to play a real role in fatherhood. So we decide that as soon as my divorce is final we will wed. The ceremony takes place in Hawaii on January 5, 1981. My son, Burt, is there as the best man. It is quiet and beautiful.

A week later, in what I would term a very unexpected wedding gift, *People* magazine prints a first-person account from Chrystie of the circumstances of our break-up, in which she writes the following:

> ...one night I was out to dinner and my friend asked me why I wanted an abortion. I told him, "I don't want the abortion." He said, "Why are you having it?" And I said, "Because Bruce wants it." He said, "You are having the abortion because the man that you are not going to be living with wants you to have it?" I thought, what an idiot I am.

I am not sure why Chrystie chose to write that. It further damaged my reputation. I also know that Casey later found out I had made the comment, which only added to the sorrow of a relationship that was never right from the start and can never be fully repaired. I was not an attentive father as she was growing up. I never felt comfortable, given the circumstances. Casey is now bright and gorgeous and an incredible mom to three children with an equally incredible husband. I know I terribly disappointed her as a father, nor was she the only child I terribly disappointed.

My marriage to Linda is short-lived, lasting only about four and a half years before we separate. Looking back now it was inevitable. Although I did not know what the term meant at that time in the early eighties, it was clear that I had gender dysphoria. It is unconscionable that I did not mention any of my issues to Linda before we were married. The failure was not malicious: there was the fear that if I had mentioned my struggles, any woman thinking of marrying me would have just run. I wanted domesticity. I wanted a family. I wanted full-time companionship. Just as I also thought that by having those things, I would exorcise what was living inside.

The ugly aspects of my personal life gone public do not help the marriage to Linda, either. They have left me tarnished: General Mills, which had originally signed me to a five-year $1 million contract after the Games with a one-year option, elects not to renew it. I still have my broadcasting career: in 1978 I moved to NBC from ABC and signed a very lucrative contract. The expectation was that I would play a pivotal role in NBC's coverage of the 1980 Olympics in Moscow. It was in my wheelhouse, a place for me to truly land, until President Carter called for the United States to boycott because of the Soviet invasion of Afghanistan.

Once again there is the question of where I am going to fit in given that the sports of football and basketball don't appeal to me. I like nontraditional sports, and I become something of an expert in hosting so-called superstar competitions, which are in vogue in the late seventies and early eighties. But I'm not sure it will be enough for NBC to keep me beyond my original contract.

My short marriage to Linda does produce two stupendous achievements: my sons Brandon and Brody. They were sublime boys then, and they are sublime men now. Brandon is an exceptional songwriter and musician who does everything well—flying helicopters, off-road biking, surfing the famed waves of Malibu, building a house. In one of the greatest athletic slaps in my life, he beat the crap out of me in table tennis as we prepared for a tournament. (I hired a ball machine to practice without telling him; he hired a world-class pro without telling me. In other words, I got punked.) I can also see in him the qualities of grace and openness he inherited from his mom and his stepfather, David.

I am also lucky that over the years my relationship with Brandon, after an unforgivable absence, has only grown stronger. He is not simply my son. He and Burt are my best friends in a life that has had few lasting close relationships.

Brody is the resident hunk, ruggedly handsome. He always has a million ideas going and is fearless in his entrepreneurship and risk—reality television star on *The Hills*, sought-after DJ.

They both are opinionated (Brandon quite, Brody not so quite). They speak with a bluntness and directness only exceeded by Burt. They are stubborn, sometimes maddeningly so. Gee, I wonder where all those qualities came from...

But they have what their father never had: they know who they are, they are comfortable with who they are, and it did not take them until the final quarter of life to even begin to like who they are.

Thank God.

For my debut role as an actor I choose the 1980 film *Can't Stop the Music*, produced by the wild and flamboyant Allan Carr. I star with Steve Guttenberg and Valerie Perrine and the Village People. I play a goofy and nerdy lawyer who somehow through a series of tortuous twists becomes the manager of a group that resembles the real-life Village People. Interspersed are scenes of Guttenberg singing and dancing for reasons that even today cannot be fully explained in terms of plot.

Carr had produced the immensely successful film *Grease* starring John Travolta and Olivia Newton-John. He had chops and a track record, not to mention raucous parties that rivaled Hefner's with Carr, who weighed over three hundred pounds, as master of ceremonies. He was hoping to cash in on the disco craze, which was hot when the movie went into production and not when the movie was in post-production. Roughly a year before the premiere was the epic Disco Demolition Night at Comiskey Park in Chicago after the first game of a White Sox double-header. The idea was for fans to bring disco records, and they would be collected and put into a crate rigged with explosives. Many of the records were never collected, and after the detonation a riot started in which records were flung about the stadium like Oddjob's hat. At least six people were injured and thirty-nine arrested.

It is safe to say that disco took a major blow after that, just as it is also safe to say that the reaction against disco, symbolized by the Village People, was not-so-veiled homophobia. It was also safe to say that the original title of the film, *Discoland—Where the Music Never Ends!*, just didn't have the same ring anymore and was changed, which made no difference when the film premiered in the United States on June 20, 1980. Nobody went to see it, although it is something of a minor cult classic and definitely worth watching in any state where it is legal to get high.

It did win a notable award, the first-ever Golden Raspberry for Worst Picture, so it did not go entirely unnoticed. I was also nominated for Worst Actor of the Year but lost out to Neil Diamond for *The Jazz Singer* in what many critics felt was an enormous upset. The reviews of me were predictable—another former athlete vainly and amateurishly trying to become an actor.

After the disaster of the film, a few other acting

opportunities come my way: when Erik Estrada, the lead actor on the NBC television show *CHiPS*, about the adventures of the California Highway Patrol, holds out for more money and threatens to quit if he doesn't get it, I am offered the job as his replacement. I like the power trip of the show: in one scene I am supposed to be directing traffic, and drivers actually think I am directing traffic. I also get to wear a very tight uniform, which I always enjoy. I do six episodes in 1981 before Estrada, realizing that the show indeed goes on without him, settles his differences with the network and returns.

I star in an NBC made-for-television movie called *Grambling's White Tiger*, based on the true story of a white quarterback playing on the legendary all-black football team at Grambling University. The film, which also stars Harry Belafonte as coach Eddie Robinson, gets excellent ratings, and I am well-received. But with the exception of a few cameo roles here and there, nothing else ever results. In the mid 1980s NBC elects not to renew my contract.

I will never know whether it was the slide of my career that caused my gender issues to inflame and make me feel desperate, or whether it was my gender issues that caused my career to slide.

I only know I am struggling with the issue of my identity more than ever in the early 1980s, so much so that I am getting uncharacteristically careless. Like the time I buy a *Cosmopolitan* magazine at a newsstand in Rockefeller Center, where NBC is headquartered, and an executive of the network sees me do it. I just ignore him as I walk by. Who knows? Maybe he is about to do the same thing anyway.

The afterglow of the Olympics, which preoccupied me and kept me going until the early 1980s, has largely burned out because I am burned out by it. I continue to do speeches and professionally race cars. But I am not locked on to anything. I have no motivation. Being a father to Burt and Casey and Brandon and Brody should sustain me. But I feel unworthy as a father, not good enough to play a major role in anyone's life.

Issues of identity have become a twenty-four-hour-a-day preoccupation. It's the same mindset as when I trained for the Olympics but without any goal or end result. All this preoccupation does is feed upon itself and make me feel worse and more insecure and confused than ever. It is inevitable when you are living a false life. You never feel comfortable. You feel like an impostor, a fraud, and there is no way you are going to have a positive image of yourself.

There is also a growing sense that by the early to mid 1980s the public, with the media as its conduit, after placing me on Mount Olympus, is now glad to see me gone. It has grown weary of me and is looking for someone else to anoint.

Live by celebrity. Die by it.

Unless maybe you are the Kardashians.

Even though we have two adorable little boys, the relationship between Linda and me is fraught with tension.

My Dad, Bill Jenner, when he was an Army Ranger in 1944. He fought in the battle of D-Day and was the toughest man I ever met. Nothing scared him. *(Original print courtesy of the Jenner family)*

At around age 2, already with good legs. I grew up in 1950s America—a period in which the country economically boomed. But it certainly wasn't an Age of Enlightenment when it came to the acceptance of others. *(Original print courtesy of the Jenner family)*

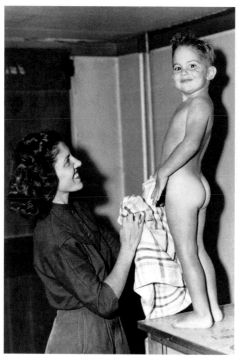

At age 3 with my mother, Esther, who has been so beautifully supportive since I transitioned. I obviously never had an issue posing for the camera. *(Original print courtesy of the Jenner family)*

With my older sister Pam in 1954. I have always idolized her, envied her, and wanted to be just like her when I was growing up. I was drawn to her closet just like I was to my mom's but could not figure out why. *(Original print courtesy of the Jenner family)*

At age 15 posing with my Dad's car, a 1960 Austin-Healey Sprite known as the "Bugeye" because of its headlights. I loved it so much that I got the same model when I became Caitlyn. *(Original print courtesy of the Jenner family)*

At 16 I knew what the status of being an athlete in high school bestows on you. Competing gave me the opportunity to deal with all the confusion I felt as a kid; to fight inferiority with superiority. *(Original print courtesy of the Jenner family)*

On the podium at the 1971 NAIA Outdoor Track & Field Championship, two years after knee surgery. My coach at Graceland University, L. D. Weldon, always told me to "just take it" in competition and in life, which became my mantra in more ways than one. *(Original print courtesy of the Jenner family)*

Pole vaulting at the 1976 Olympics. It was always my favorite event. I liked the freedom and spiraling aloneness. *(Heinz Kluetmeier/Getty Images)*

Right after winning the men's decathlon. It was such a great moment for me, for my family, and for my country. But I also knew in an instant that my life would change forever. The Grand Diversion was over, and I had been christened overnight as the ultimate American Male Athlete. *(Ed Lacey/Popperfoto/Getty Images)*

With Chrystie right after winning. I never would have made it to the Olympics if it weren't for her. We quickly became the "Golden Couple." *(Neil Leifer/Getty Images)*

Posing with the gold medal hanging around my neck. The morning after, I looked in the mirror and thought, "Now that it's over, who am I?" *(Bettmann / Getty Images)*

My brother Burt's 1976 graduation photo. He was going to join Chrystie and me in California shortly after graduation. We were just getting to know each other. *(Original print courtesy of the Jenner family)*

Posing for a photo shoot at my home in Malibu with my dog Bertha in 1980. I did hundreds of these as I became a media personality after the Olympics. *(John G. Zimmerman/Getty Images)*

At the *Can't Stop the Music* 1980 premiere with Linda. This was early on in our relationship, before our two kids were born and well before I told her about my gender dysphoria. *(Images Press/ Getty Images)*

On the set of *CHiPS* in 1981 with Erik Estrada (left) and Larry Wilcox (right) where I played Officer Steve McLeish for six episodes. My foray into acting never really went anywhere. I wonder if my sliding career caused my gender issues to inflame, or if it was my preoccupation with my gender issues that caused me to let my career slide. *(NBC/NBCU Photo Bank via Getty Images)*

Doing a "bit" with Bob Hope and Merlin Olsen as "the Melody Maids" at a 1981 Bob Hope comedy special. Although appearing in drag was supposed to be a gag, in actuality it became something of a godsend for me. I was careful to not seem too comfortable, so I tried to play with it and be cool. The gag wasn't memorable. But I did get out of it a great pair of heels that actually fit me. *(NBC/NBCU Photo Bank via Getty Images)*

I am not only frustrated with the relationship but also frustrated with myself, depressed and ashamed of the mess I have made. One marriage is over; another one is going downhill. I'm trying to participate in the raising of four children under the age of eight and not doing a very good job of it.

We bicker. I am moody, the kind of moodiness that comes when you are yearning to be someone and something different, this fire inside you that only gets hotter and hotter with no real escape.

I seek every opportunity I can to cross-dress. It is a temporary fix, like it always is. You feel a rush of adrenaline and then you feel as sad and deflated as ever, play-acting when you don't want to play and don't want to act anymore. But something is still better than nothing.

I get my hands on a couple of wigs. There is a light brown one that I think suits me. I begin to wonder what I would look like on camera. That would be kind of cool. So I get the little recorder we have and a tripod and I set it up in the bedroom. I shoot into the mirror so I can see my reflection: it makes the lighting on my face better if I position the camera a certain way. I also want to see how I walk—if I can adopt any fluidity at all and not the prototypical bowlegged on-the-balls-of-your-feet jock walk—and do several takes. I am having a real ball now, more fun than I have had for a long time. I play the video back. It is the first time I have seen myself in anything but a mirror. I look to some degree like a man who decides to wear a dress when the wife and kids are away. I *am* a man who decides to wear a dress when his wife and kids are away. But I don't see that. I don't see Bruce Jenner in a dress.

I see me.

I should erase the tape. There is too much risk of Linda finding it no matter how well I hide it: wives find everything anyway. But I can't. This little glimpse of me is too important, too vital, to let go of.

Now I at least know.

If only for an instant.

Maybe if I tell Linda, it will be better. Maybe if I stop the lies and the deceit, show her that Bruce is just a façade, I won't feel this pent up, pacing back and forth in my cage. It's not like Bruce is particularly thriving at this point in his life. The highs are coming fewer and farther between. In fact, they are not coming at all.

So tell Linda. She is your wife. She is the mother of two of your children. Doesn't she have the right to know? To understand why you are so angry all the time, as if it is only her fault?

I tell her.

She doesn't understand. How could she in the context of the early 1980s, not only because gender identity is a foreign concept in the public mainstream but also because this is Bruce Jenner standing in front of her? The man she thought was a hunk when she and Elvis lay in bed and watched him win the decathlon (Elvis thought the same thing). The man she thought was the ultimate in macho and still thinks so.

Now you are telling her that you identify as a woman? That you have cheated on her in the most unimaginable way possible by concealing your identity?

Linda, to her credit, does want to understand. We eventually go together to a therapist, and she grapples with the concept of gender dysphoria. She wonders if it is temporary, something that goes away. The therapist is emphatic: never. It is only a matter of how you deal with it.

Linda and I struggle on. It isn't that I don't love her. It is bigger than that: I don't love myself. We both know our marriage is almost certainly over, but I tell her to meet me in New York, where I am making an appearance, so we can spend some time together. It gives her hope that maybe the marriage can be saved. There *still* is love and our two beautiful boys.

She knocks on the door of the hotel room where I am staying.

I open it.

I am in a dress and wig and makeup.

Linda says nothing.

I am not sure what I was thinking then, and I am not entirely sure thirty years later. I know I was terribly frustrated and irritable. Maybe I was blaming Linda for not letting me live my life when in fact I had never told her about my life until we had been married for several years.

Maybe I wanted the marriage to end and this was the sure-fire way to do it. Or maybe after telling Linda I felt compelled that she now actually meet the woman inside me.

I had to try.

I realize I have done something terrible by putting her in this situation. I will never forget that look of shock and hurt on her face. I *have* hurt her, and she does not deserve it.

I guess this isn't working out.

Perhaps the greatest understatement of all time.

I run into the bathroom and immediately change. I walk back out.

I am so sorry.

I mean the words. But I know they mean nothing. Because at this stage of my life there is nothing that means anything.

Linda is silent.

I am done, except to work as little as I have to and disappear the rest of the time. I won't kill myself, because I am not that kind of person. But maybe I should. Maybe it would be better for everyone, most of all me. Within a decade after the Olympics, after all the glory and honor and so proudly embracing the flag of my country as I took a victory lap and could have taken a hundred more, I am in a place I never ever thought I would be.

I am alone.

—◊—

November 12, 2015

*"I went to school there. I got my degree there.
I never wore heels there."*

I am on the road to Lamoni.

Every encounter, every event, still feels new and unpre-
dictable as I approach my eight-month anniversary after
transitioning. It isn't about how I emotionally feel inside,
because I am already at ease with myself. The roles have
most definitely switched, Caitlyn on the outside and Bruce
on the inside, where he will happily remain for the rest
of my days.

When you are dealing with your gender identity, the
intensity of the experience is different in every person.
Some know right away at an early age that the gender
they are living as is not their gender. For some it's a longer
process of discovery. Some never know, which is why the
labels of *female* and *male* will one day no longer be applica-
ble. Because that's all they are anyway, labels that narrow
experience instead of expanding it. The same goes for the

label of *trans*. Right now we are inevitably referred to as a trans woman or a trans man. But I predict that in the next generation there will be no qualifiers, that we are women and men or whatever we wish to call ourselves, blending into society instead of being stigmatized as some fringe trans species. The less people notice us, other than that we are fun and interesting and as "normal" as anyone else out there, the more we will know we have been accepted.

We aren't there yet because of our obsession with male and female. I never felt I was whole. It was almost like I was two people. I could live in the male world and did, but from birth there was always this woman inside me. She never went away, yet for so long I could not let her live, given the times and what I came to symbolize.

Until now.

Returning to Graceland almost forty-five years after graduation in 1973 is going to be a little bit different.

I went to school there. I got my degree there. I never wore heels there.

Several of those who coached me will be there today. Will the image they once had now be obliterated? Will they see me for who I am, or will they see some knock-off, not Caitlyn Jenner in a white pantsuit, but Bruce Jenner in a white pantsuit?

I understand if they feel that way. It would kill me, but I would still understand. The idea that everyone instantly feels at home with Caitlyn is absurd. It may take a day.

It may take a week or a year, or it might never take at all. Getting upset because somebody uses the pronoun *he* instead of *she* when first meeting me is ridiculous. In the beginning after transition, even I began to write out "Bruce" when I signed checks. It is confusing, particularly for those who knew me as Bruce, and many millions did. Plus, seeing me as Caitlyn on television or in the pages of a magazine is totally different than seeing me in the flesh. There is no distance or filter or running for the hills or spitting in disgust or thinking this is just another Kardashian caper for maximum publicity.

After speaking to dozens of trans women and men over the past months, it is clear that an assumption is made that everything about us has radically changed overnight. We *have* radically changed, but we still retain many of our core beliefs, or at least I have. I *am* different than I was. I *feel* different and I *look* different, but I am not as different in personality as is sometimes assumed. It is often hard to convince people of that, which is why they are nervous and I am nervous, plus I also hope I made the right clothing choice.

Before we get to Graceland we have to get to Chicago. I am here with the six other transgender women who are regulars on the second season of *I Am Cait*. I am giving a speech to benefit Chicago House, a service organization that is providing remarkable support to the LGBTQ community and those impacted by HIV/AIDS by facilitating housing, employment, and legal services. Then the seven of us will board a bus and wind our way through parts of Iowa and eventually down to New Orleans.

A handheld megaphone blares in the cold of the windy city outside the Chicago Hilton Hotel after I am finished. The words are sharp and angry.

We don't get jobs. We don't get any money. It isn't all fun and games. You don't care about the real trans women of America. You get those awards and dress up, but you have no idea what it's really like.

We don't need you, we don't want you. You don't speak for us. We didn't ask for your help. Do you have any idea of what is happening out here?

You have no right to represent us. You are an insult.

You are an insult to trans people.

A clueless rich white woman.

We have been assaulted by police. We have been assaulted by johns. We have been violated. We have been violated by the system.

How many sixty-five-year-old white women get killed?

I have heard variations on these themes so many times before it has become a mantra: I don't represent the trans community. I am an insult to the trans community. I am a clueless rich white woman.

I don't know what to do but say it again. And again. And again.

I have worked hard. I have been successful. Yes, I am white and privileged. And yes, I am a trans woman.

I am not trying to act as if I am the Mother Teresa

THE SECRETS OF MY LIFE

of the transgender community. But I am trying to learn as much as I can as quickly as I can. I am meeting other trans women and trans men and parents of teenagers whose children transitioned and were mercilessly bullied for it and daughters whose fathers were too afraid to express their true selves and talking with them and using my show as a worldwide platform.

But yes, talk is sometimes cheap, so I continue to raise money for the trans community because I have the platform to do so, working with corporations with a global presence. I am currently working with MAC to sell a lipstick online under my name called Finally Free. One hundred percent of the proceeds goes to the MAC Aids Fund Transgender Initiative. So far we've raised $1.3 million that has been distributed to organizations working on behalf of transgender women and men all over the world. I deserve no pat on the back. All of us can do things large and small. We must remain united and strong to fight and make change.

I believe I know where the protest is coming from. I believe I know who they represent at least partially: African American trans women who are turned down for jobs because of prejudice and are forced to work the streets as sex workers to make a living and often jeopardize their lives. I know the tragic syndrome that too often exists and is little spoken of: a trans woman has sex with a john; words of hate get out in the community that the john supposedly just had sex with a guy who thinks he is a woman but still has a penis so it is perceived as an act of homosexuality; teasing and ridicule follow; the john kills the transgender woman he had sex with to save face and avoid further humiliation and to assert what he thinks is his manhood. Too many trans women's lives don't seem to have meaning in our society. Police investigations into their murders are often perfunctory. If a case gets to court, the sentence for the killer is often too light and the hate crime statute is rarely invoked.

I know that as I speak in November 2015 there have been a record twenty-two killings so far this year of transgender or gender nonconforming people, all but three of which—*three*—were of black or Latinos (the killings will continue at a record rate in 2016). I know of the fear that exists on Six Mile and Woodward in Detroit, or on Santa Monica and Vine in Hollywood. I know Kiesha Jenkins was attacked and shot dead by a group of young men in Philadelphia on October 6, 2015. I know that Tamara Dominguez was run over several times by a truck in Kansas City on August 15.

Can I identify with these victims or any other victim of violence? Of course not. Can I feel horrible pain for them? Yes. Have I talked to those who have been victims? Yes. Do I believe that more has to be done to label these acts of violence as hate crimes? Yes. Am I concerned that police may have a bias against transgender women who work the street? Yes. Do we have to fight through prejudice to help our trans women get jobs? Yes. Should we stop the bullshit and make it effortlessly easy in *every* state for a transgender woman or man to get their gender marker changed on official forms such as birth certificates and driver's licenses so there is absolutely no question of what gender they are when they apply for jobs? Yes.

I have absolutely no malice toward the protester with the megaphone. I want to talk to her. I want to hear her story. I want to know more about what I could and should do. I reach out to touch her and hear somebody else scream:

Don't you fucking touch her! Don't you fucking touch her!

I still want to talk to her. I still want her to know me a little bit, hear my heart, look into my eyes, even if she does wear a scarf around her face so I will never be able to look directly into hers.

I think about not being able to reach the protester as the bus heads from Chicago to Lamoni. I even try to get her name, but it is a lost cause. I have to let it go because Graceland is now looming ahead.

I look out the window as the bus goes down College Avenue. There's Patroness Hall and the Floyd McDowell Commons and the Helene Center for the Visual Arts and the Shaw Center. We stop at the Bruce Jenner Sports Complex, which in the aftermath of my Olympic success was named after me. A small plaque still hangs in the lobby showing me in a red warm-up jacket with black stripes down the sides with the gold medal draped around my neck. My accomplishments are duly noted in black type on an appropriately gold background. I am smiling, but it is a thin smile, almost uncertain, or at least hesitant. Something is off, maybe because I showed the smile so many times when I received plaques. While I was honored to receive them, I also knew they were becoming increasingly meaningless. I wonder now if that smile had become a transparent mask for inner guilt and maybe even embarrassment that I really didn't deserve this plaque or the gold medal or anything else.

So I smiled. It was all I could do.

Just try to smile.

Some of the buildings look exactly the same. Some have been modernized. Some are new. But the feel is still of a small and humble college of brick and mortar dedicated to its students and, as a church-affiliated school, encouraging a moral life. But whose morals and by what standard? Those who condemn transgender men and women use religion as a cudgel, saw, and machete. The God they see is not benevolent but cruel and vindictive and relentlessly judgmental. They see no beauty in the Bible, only blasphemy.

Yet another reason for my nervousness: what vision of God will emerge when we take the stage, the kind and merciful one or the one hell-bent on destroying me and my fellow trans sisters?

Minutes before I take the stage I see one of my old Graceland football coaches, Jerry Hampton. He has been associated with Graceland for close to seventy years as a student and coach and teacher. He personifies the roots of the school and the kind of sanctuary it provided to a kid from the east looking for something to latch on to. He coached football for twenty-five years, tennis for thirty-three years, and wrestling for twenty-two years (his teams were never defeated in dual meets or tournaments).

I want to renew the goodwill that we felt toward one another when we were here from 1968 to 1973. I suddenly become self-conscious. Is my hair okay? Did I put too much makeup on? Is a white pantsuit too conservative? Should I have stuck to basic black? Or maybe just jeans and a shirt so as to not look too polished?

Maybe Coach Hampton won't care about the clothes at all. Maybe it will be the disappointment in seeing me no matter how much he tries to hide it, recognizing me from pictures but unable to recognize who I have become. He was my coach, and it is not every day that male athletes who go on to win the Olympics come back as a woman. Jerry offers a glowing smile when he sees me, a prodigal son coming home, if only for a few hours, one who at this point in time should probably be referred to as a prodigal daughter. The smile from Jerry says it all: he gets what I did, and it makes no difference. The link between us, a former player with the former coach, is strong and timeless.

"You're still here!" I say when I see him, which could be misinterpreted to suggest surprise and shock that he is still alive. I don't mean it that way. I am just surprised he is still at Graceland after all these years. Tact is not necessarily my strong suit.

"We were bragging on you in my office," the president of the school, John Sellars, tells me. "We were talking about you as a student and how proud they are of you."

As a student?

Fine revisionist history.

We walk into the packed auditorium. The applause is loud, a good sign. "Today Graceland students have a great opportunity to have a discussion about gender identity," says assistant professor Raquel Moreira in introducing us. "There are no wrong questions. You ask what you feel you should ask."

How did you go about keeping up your transformation and still acknowledging God in your life?

An honest question well put. It was during a conversation with my pastor about God, and whether he or she would still embrace me, that gave me the courage to transition.

"I got this one," says the one and only Chandi, commandeering the microphone with one of her patented *don't fuck with me here* stare-downs. I look at her. She doesn't look at me. Her eyes are steely, looking straight ahead. Chandi, who has become one of my fellow sisters on *I Am Cait* and a great friend, is strong. Chandi brooks no bullshit. Chandi is funny. Chandi is loving. Chandi is an activist. Chandi is outspoken, *very* outspoken. She has been in the trenches of the trans community for all those years. She has lived it and continues to live it every day.

146

The question from the student, gentle on the surface, does raise the issue of how God can be in your life when you are a trans woman or man and what you have done is perceived as repugnant and indecent and shameful.

Chandi, remember this is my alma mater.

Protesters screaming at me in Chicago were bad enough.

Well, it actually was hard. I grew up in a very religious family. Many years I heard that my life was an abomination, so I lost touch with God for many years. I had to recognize the fact that God knew who I was before I did, so how can I be falling out of touch with God when he knew before I did? It's a connection I've made that now that I have, I will never let it go again.

She receives vigorous applause. It is a beautiful articulation of what I feel and perhaps many other transgender women and men feel, the cycle of rejection and shame and then the blessing of acceptance. It came for Chandi. It came for me. But it does not come easily for others, whether it's religion or friends or family.

The words of Kate Bornstein, who speaks next, open my eyes to how lucky I have been to get the acceptance I have gotten and how much of it has come from my station of privilege and celebrity.

Like 99.9 percent of men and women who transition, she had no public relations expert advising her on how to do it. She did what she did with the knowledge that the bonds of family might irreparably rupture.

Another of my sisters on the show, Kate is a year and

a half older than me. She has become something of a den mother as I navigate my way, a product of her wisdom and maturity and my insulation in the world of white male privilege.

We relate on a keen emotional level, perhaps because she, too, has had her entanglements with the trans community and refuses to back down. In 1986 she had gender-affirming surgery to become Kate. But she refuses to strictly label herself as a woman and thinks gender labels are a social and medical construct. Her book *Gender Outlaw* is funny, smart, and provocative without in-your-face provocation. One passage in particular is worth repeating because of her honest clarity, trying to sort out the very concept of man becoming woman and woman becoming man and whether it is truly possible:

> I know I'm not a man—about that much I'm very clear, and I've come to the conclusion that I'm probably not a woman either, at least not according to a lot of people's rules on this sort of thing. The trouble is, we're living in a world that insists we be one or the other—a world that doesn't bother to tell us exactly what one or the other is.

She calls herself and other trans women and men "trannys." It has been met with fury by some who think it reinforces the terrible misperception that we are merely playing dress-up, men who wear women's clothing and women who wear men's clothing. She does it out of affection. It is a word, not a condemnation. She is trying to take some of the sanctimony out of the sails of the trans community, to let them know that it is okay to have a sense of humor while not dismissing the horrible inequities and tragedies that still exist.

Because you still feel pain in Kate. You still see moments where she is haunted.

She was born into a seemingly perfect nuclear family, growing up in New Jersey in the 1950s—doctor dad, mom who had trained as a teacher, two sons. Kate went to an all-boys school, where the combination of being overweight and Jewish made her an easy target for the viciousness of her peers. She then went on to Brown University, where she discovered a talent for performance. But as she struggled with gender she also struggled with spirituality and whether there was a place that would accept her. She tried the Amish church and Kabbalah and then Scientology.

Scientology seems so totally ill-suited for Kate, given her gender issues. I don't understand why she did it. I am not sure she understands why she did it, and even when she explains it I am still not sure she understands why she did it. Except that when you are struggling with gender, in Kate's case knowing she was not a man but unsure she was a woman, you reach for whatever distraction you can, the more intense the distraction the better. But it became hell.

Right before she left she said she was placed on a lie detector for six hours in an attempt to pinpoint her gender identity. She was excommunicated, leaving behind a daughter, whom Kate has not seen for more than thirty years. As she tells the audience:

My daughter is a high-ranking executive in the church of Scientology. To Scientologists my trans-ness is proof that I am an evil person and should not be talked with. So I haven't seen her since she was nine. She is now forty-two, forty-three years old.

Tears are forming in her eyes. You can feel the pain that will never go away. It isn't just Kate missing out. It is also her daughter denying herself the pleasure of knowing this kind and remarkable woman—performer, subtle activist without stridency, tolerant of anyone and everyone, gentle, so very gentle, and now grappling with a recurrence of cancer.

She says to the audience that she has not given up the hope of seeing her daughter. But I think she has. I think in her heart is the realization she will never see her again. This is so often the price of becoming a transgender man or woman, something so precious and sacred lost as something so sacred and precious is gained.

She leaves the students with this, as simple as it is complicated, as complicated as it simple:

Look for the heart of the doctrine you are following. If it is at all mean, think twice before following it any further.

—◊—

Chapter Seven

Zap Zap Zap

ELECTROLYSIS

Plural electrolyses \-sez\

1a: the destruction of hair roots by an electrologist
by means of an electric current applied to the
body with a needle-shaped electrode

b: something that hurts unimaginably

c: I deserve it

Here's the clinical description of how my beard is removed
after I move into a tiny house in Malibu in the mid 1980s
in my self-imposed exile.

The licensed practitioner, known as the electrologist,
takes a metal probe of anywhere from 0.002 to 0.006
inch in diameter and slides it into the hair follicle and

the locus of where the hair is formed, what in technical terms is known as the hair matrix. Electricity is transmitted through the probe, first at the lowest setting possible and then increasing, depending on how easy it is to cause sufficient damage to prevent future growth.

There are several methods: galvanic, in which anywhere from zero to three milliamperes is applied in a constant current of voltage and a killing agent of sodium hydroxide is formed at the hair matrix; thermolysis, in which the hair matrix cells are heated with the probe anywhere from 118 degrees Fahrenheit to 122 degrees Fahrenheit to kill them off; and the blend method, in which aspects of galvanic and thermolysis are combined.

In other words, it hurts like hell.

Now consider that there are approximately 30,000 hairs in the average man's beard. Further consider that many of these hairs are deeply embedded. Also consider that the average length of a session is three hours, and multiply that by weekly sessions for at least two years. Finally consider that each removal is associated with sharp pricking and burning and throbbing.

For me that's not enough.

I refuse to use any oral or topical analgesics that can significantly reduce the pain. I don't like painkillers of any kind. I never used them—or any drugs—when training for the decathlon because I didn't like the feeling they caused over my body, a loss of control.

So this is a form of torture, willing torture. I hate the

pain, but I deserve the pain. I deserve it because of who I am, a freak without a home, trapped between the male world and the female world, a hostage of the fame and celebrity and remuneration that has come my way because of the popular perception of my very maleness. If my body looked different when I won the Olympics and wasn't rippled with muscles, if my face looked different, if my name was different and not the easy cadence of one syllable and then two, if I had won any event at the Olympics other than the decathlon, none of this would have happened. It's bizarre to consider this, the impact of all these different attributes coming together. Millions look up to me and respect me and maybe envy me. All I can say is don't: I hate myself with each passing day and take pain not only because I think I deserve it but because maybe it's the only way I can feel anything at this point in my life in the mid 1980s.

Still in my mid thirties, I am twice divorced. I have become an increasingly distant father to my four children, so consumed and self-absorbed by my gender dysphoria and the increasing realization that I must transition. Sometimes I just want to literally rip the skin off me. Get out of this ridiculous costume of flesh and bone. I feel like I am living on borrowed time with my kids, the contemplation of becoming someone they will not recognize.

I am watching television but I am not really paying attention, maybe because I find myself unable to pay attention to anything. The channels click absently, and I stop at a news segment featuring the executive director of an organization in Orange County that offers services for transgender men and women. I don't even know there is such an organization. So I call information and ask for the number. I talk to the person I saw on the news. I tell him I have a lot of gender issues and ask if he can give me a referral for any therapists in the Los Angeles area. He obviously doesn't know who I am, and more obviously he doesn't care.

Sure, I can help.

He gives me the names of two men and a woman. Because of my eternal discomfort with men I choose the woman. Her name is Gertrude Hill. She is doing sessions out of her house in the Encino area in the Valley, and I make an appointment. I drive out there and I am scared to death. But I am also excited at the prospect of letting go of all this, getting it all out, years and years of pent-up feelings finally exploding. I will see her in individual therapy for the next five years up until 1990 as she helps me through the darkest period of my life.

The first thing I notice about her is that she is about a foot shorter than I am, maybe closer to a foot and a half. She has a thick Jewish accent and is Dr. Ruthian in appearance and manner, in her early fifties at the time. There is an inordinate sensitivity to her. I sense she has been through something that has given her uncommon empathy for people. Later on I find out why.

Born in Hungary, she and her mother were rounded up

by the Nazis and taken to Auschwitz when she was eleven in 1944. Her father had been taken away two weeks earlier and perished. When they were herded from the railroad car at the concentration camp, a Jewish capo, knowing that mothers and daughters were immediately marked for the gas chamber, pulled Trudy aside:

Don't say to anyone that this is your mother. Stay clear. You are not a child anymore.

She stayed near her mother but never beside her. During her five months there a mother killed her newborn baby so she would not be turned in. The deceased infant was then given to Trudy for disposal.

Someone handed me something dirty and messy and mushy in my hands and said, "Bury it."

She and her mother were then transported to two different concentration camps, Salzwedel and Bergen-Belsen, before their liberation by Allied forces in April 1945.

Trudy never lost her faith in God, which is of tremendous solace to me because there have been so many times I am convinced that God has lost faith in me. The more I see Trudy and get to know her, the more it becomes clear that she has made gender dysphoria her specialty to alleviate the pain and suffering of others who feel like they have no place else to turn. Somehow she had converted the inhumanity of the camps into her own humanity.

The first thing Trudy gives me is desperately needed perspective, that the feelings inside me are not abnormal and there are many others who have them. She wants to try to pinpoint the full extent. She puts me through a series of psychological tests and questionnaires. The only one I remember is the Rorschach, where everything looks like a butterfly. Based on those tests the diagnosis is clear: I am gender dysphoric—she explains the term so I fully understand it for the first time—and am a woman inside.

This is the way you are. It will never go away.

Is there any cure for this?

No. It's only a matter of how you deal with it.

How do I deal with it? By denying it? Been there, done that. I am extraordinarily lonely. I don't fit in anywhere. There is no place for me. I have let go of pretty much everyone I know. I feel increasingly estranged from my mom: after watching her go through the death of Burt, there is no way I am going to unload this on her.

I do tell Pam somewhere in this period of the early to mid 1980s. I will never forget her reaction, no matter how much she tried to understand: her eyes were so glazed by shock that it was like she did not recognize me. Neither will Pam:

Bruce was still Bruce then. He called me and said he was in Miami, where I lived, and that he wanted to have dinner. I said that sounds great, let me check with my husband at the time, Bill. He said, "no no no, I want to talk to you about a family matter."

It was extremely rare, but it did not send up any red flags at the time. I thought it had maybe to do with his marriage. We went to a restaurant and made small talk for a while and he said, "I have something to tell you. I have always felt like a woman."

I couldn't even understand what he was saying at the time. He said, "When we were young I used to go in and try your clothes on and sometimes Mom's." I am just dumbfounded. I can't believe what I am hearing. He said, "I really think I need to do something about it." I can't remember how I responded.

I do remember my drive home, and I am crying so hard I can hardly see the road. Sobbing and sobbing. For several reasons. One was selfishly: "My famous brother who I idolize is thinking about becoming a woman?" Then I started to think about his pain for all those years. This was a new person in front of me. I had a very hard time sharing it with anybody. I didn't even tell my husband. It was our secret.

Most of all I feel estranged from my dad. But every time I play out the conversation, it turns out differently. He can accept it. He can't accept it. He won't accept it.

I'm not Bruce, Dad. I never really was.

Then who the hell are you?

I saw those tears of joy fall down his cheeks when I sought him out in the stands after winning the Olympics. It was as if I could feel them on my own face.

What would he think now?

You're not a goddamn woman! You're my son. You're Bruce. Snap out of it, for chrissakes. You're talking nonsense.

My self-imposed isolation unit is the Malibu shack, in an area known as Point Dume (trust me, you can't make this stuff up). It is small with a galley kitchen and an open living room upstairs and two bedrooms downstairs. The so-called master bedroom is claustrophobic, so I put my bed in the living room, which has sliding doors and a good view. I use one of the downstairs bedrooms for my growing collection of women's clothing. My mom visits me once, sees them, and is happy I have a girlfriend.

Wendy Roth, a coordinating producer for *Good Morning America*, where I worked as a field reporter, has purchased many of them for me. Wendy has become my confidante, the person I trust the most and have told the most until I go into therapy. Unlike anyone else, as far as I know, she did think something was astray:

I knew something was off. Because he wasn't your typical macho guy. He wasn't, like, going after women. He wasn't very sociable. He wasn't living the celeb life that he could have been leading. He didn't feel sorry for himself. I never got that sense. I just got the sense that he wanted to be somebody else. And we often talked about it—"why don't you just go away"—but then there was also the whole thing of how do you support yourself and does somebody who is well-known just disappear.

I speak to Wendy almost every day during various periods in the 1980s. I sometimes talk for an hour straight and she listens, she actually listens.

She sees in me embedded qualities that I have lost sight of because of my self-loathing: kindness, generosity, somebody fun to be around. She knows that I like big and expensive toys (Porsches and planes). But she also knows that I couldn't really care less about money. By Malibu standards the Malibu shack is actually more of an outhouse. Hey, I'm cool with that: the water runs, there actually is a toilet and it flushes, and there are no leaks.

Wendy is based in New York but travels to Los Angeles on a regular basis. When we are together we go shopping—a dress, maybe, or some lingerie. When a salesperson asks if we need help, we tell them we are shopping for Wendy and she has dragged me along. All the salesperson has to do is look at us to know the story is suspect—Wendy could almost fit in the back pocket of my pants so an extra large would envelop her—but at least we are left alone. Later on, to make the story more plausible, we tell the salespeople we are shopping for a friend. Sometimes Wendy just goes out on her own, buying me wigs because she thinks the ones I mail-order are cheap and crappy and ill-fitting, which they are. Later on, as my marriage to Kris is dying in 2013 and I ultimately move out, I open a debit card account in Wendy's name and deposit money into it so she can buy clothing for me online without anything being billed directly to me.

There are stretches in the mid 1980s where I stay inside the shack for a week, except to get food. Dishes pile up. I am never going to get an A for dusting and vacuuming. The place is an embarrassment for someone who signed the million-dollar deal with General Mills and the very generous contract with NBC and can still give corporate speeches. But there is the familiar refrain I repeat over and over in my life. I say it once, I say it a thousand times:

I don't really care.

Once again I do not contemplate suicide, but I sometimes wonder what the difference is when you are hollow inside and nothing matters and you can't make a connection to anyone. You never feel on even ground, emotional calm and then the street begins to buckle: emboldened to transition and take the step, then terrified. So eager to be authentic, then incapable. Knowing what you should do but not doing it.

Remember this?

He simply is a real-life version of the American dream, fairly bursting with honest vitality, infectious health and cheerful good humor. Is it his fault that he's direct, self-assured, sincere? The type of person we'd all like to be when we grow up?

—KENNETH TURAN, *THE WASHINGTON POST*

Maybe I owe the world a correction.

When I first start seeing Trudy, it doesn't take long for

her to sense my misery. She reinforces that I am not the only person struggling with such conflict and feelings. The concept of gender dysphoria is no longer alien. It is in her office that for the first time in my life I see a transgender woman face-to-face. We are having a session and it is winding down and a little light goes on to indicate that the next patient is in the waiting room. Trudy mentions that the patient is a trans woman and without giving me her name or any other identifying characteristic, wonders if I might simply like to see her. I go into the waiting room and grab a magazine and don't dare talk to her. My initial reaction is so similar to how much of the public reacts now to a trans person.

I feel nervous. I feel shy. But she seems so comfortable with herself. Is that what happens when you transition? You actually become comfortable with yourself? You can just blend in?

Trudy's underlying goal was to help me come to terms with myself in whatever way I defined it, and as hard as it was, to not be trapped by the expectations of others. Because that is not a life. It is the pose of a life.

Without directly saying it, I can tell that for my own personal welfare she thinks I must take some actual steps to physically feel more myself. Since there is no cure for this, I have to deal with it on my own terms, as is true for anyone with gender dysphoria. They are little things that I think I can get away with, nothing like facial feminization surgery and certainly not the Final Surgery. I am not ready for any of that and may never be.

Since at this I point I am driving around a little bit at night anyway I decide to meet Trudy at her office, now in Beverly Hills. I have a long skirt on and a nice top. A cute little outfit if I say so myself and I do. I park my car half a block from her office. I sense the lights of a vehicle shining on my back. It drives right by as if nothing happened. It reminds me of back when I was a little boy in Tarrytown walking around Sleepy Hollow Gardens but with a slightly different sensation.

How nice is that? I just blend in. How cool is that?

I go to Trudy's office and she tells me I look great. She suggests dinner. But that's too much for me. I couldn't even use my voice to order, way too recognizable. I can just see the furtive smiles as they look at me and then glance away and elbow their dinner companions to sneak a look *but be careful don't let him know!* The self-consciousness will cause me to want to run away and never stop.

One step at a time.

It's all I can do.

I hate my beard. It is revolting to me, clean-shaven in the morning and then all those nubby black bristles back by nighttime like unwanted ants. It is the same with the hair on my legs, which I begin to regularly wax.

Trudy provides information on electrolysis. It is common for someone in the process of transitioning to have his beard removed. She helps me find a qualified technician I remember only as Olga. She has a house near Los Angeles International Airport with a back room that has an examining table and equipment. I walk in the first time with three or four days of growth. I want her to think that it's simply irritating and I hate shaving. But I am pretty sure she has worked on clients taking steps of transition. She knows who I am, but she never asks. She is a consummate professional.

I can only handle two hours at a time because the pain is so terrible. It is like getting a shot in your face with the needle pretty far down into the skin—okay, it hurts, but I can handle it—and then Olga hits a button with her foot to set off the electric charge and now you are at DEFCON 1. The shock only lasts for a millisecond. So you try to tell yourself the worst is over when you are zapped again and again and again. Plus after every shock she tweezes the follicle out. In some areas it may take four or five treatments to get all the hair out. I also have decided to go all the way down to the neck and chest. Pull out every hair, Olga. Every goddamn one.

There is numbing cream you can apply as well as oral medication. Anyone in his right mind would use them, but I never even bring the subject up. I lie there with tears in my eyes after each dig and zap and pull. The upper lip and around the nose are the worst of all, but I still lie there and take it.

Olga works quickly, the only merciful part of the ordeal. She charges forty dollars an hour and never raises her prices, but even so the entire cost can be upward of $30,000.

Olga and I are a year and a half in before potential

disaster strikes. I am early for an appointment and park down the block as usual to avoid detection. But another client apparently sees me on the street, and the next time he starts asking questions.

Was that Bruce Jenner down there?

Olga covers for me and denies it. I am grateful to her. She tells me that the client who saw me is a transgender woman.

Well, you know, I have my own gender issues.

I kind of figured that.

You become friendly with someone who pulls your hair follicles out week after week. There is a certain intimacy there, although I think there are probably better ways to achieve that intimacy. When you are not trying to reduce the pain medically, talking is the only antidote. So we chat about everything else—kids, what's new, life—but never the trans issue except for that one mention.

Olga is almost finished when she tells me she is moving to San Diego. I panic a little bit, because there are some areas that need to be touched up, but then I figure out what I will do.

I have always loved flying and have owned a plane of one kind or another since the Olympics. As a kid I remember going to nearby Westchester County Airport and just watching them as they took off, wondering where they were going, trying to imagine what it would be like to go anywhere you wanted without traffic lights or stop lights or arguments over directions. What joy there must be in that. What freedom. I never thought I would own a plane, because I never thought I would have enough money. I dated a girl in high school whose dad owned a plane. It was the coolest thing ever, and I stuck around in the relationship longer than I should have just so I could hear some of his flying stories. I cannot be sure, but I think she finally realized that I liked her dad's plane more than I liked her. So she dumped me.

Shortly after the Olympics, I had enough money to buy my first plane. The sensation was exactly what I expected, up in the air in the one place where I could be alone and not feel alone.

Now, in the 1980s, I own a Beechcraft Baron, but because of the financial situation I am in, I won't be able to afford it much longer. Nevertheless, for the next month or so I fly to San Diego. Olga immediately picks me up and we drive to her house. It's easier now and only takes about an hour, just a little *zap zap zap* where the hair has grown back. She drives me back to the airport after she is finished. I fly home. Nobody knows a thing, all very cloak and dagger. I feel like the James Bond of electrolysis.

I hate my nose. I have always hated my nose. It has a kind of Bob Hope ski jump look going. I want a smaller nose. A cute one. I go to a plastic surgeon in Beverly Hills and give him the spiel: I can't stand my nose so I am wondering if you can take the hook out of it. He does it, but in my mind he doesn't do it very well, which—along with the electrolysis—only arouses whispers down the line in the media that Bruce Jenner is looking a little weird these days.

Then comes hormone therapy.

It is an enormous decision. There certainly will be significant physical changes, including the development of breasts and some loss of muscle definition. Hair also grows at a slower rate, which means less electrolysis. Avoiding detection will ultimately become more difficult than ever—hiding breasts is not for the faint of heart—but living with myself as Bruce is a million times harder. The woman inside me needs estrogen to blossom. I have to feed the beast, so to speak, and since I obviously cannot produce it myself I need an alternative. I am now determined to fully transition before I turn forty in 1989. I want to have some life left. I don't want to do it when I am old. I am also now actively considering facial feminization surgery, a lengthy procedure to reconfigure the face that can take as long as ten hours. Now that I know so much more, I am thinking about the Final Surgery as well.

During my therapy with Trudy, she asks me for my ultimate fantasy. The first thing that comes to me is being fully transitioned and walking down a California beach absolutely free. Free from all the inner struggles. Peace in my soul. Free to really be me without anyone caring.

Which is why I am almost afraid to bring up the issue of hormone therapy with her. In my soul I want to do it. But am I crazy? I am still a celebrity, even if I am tarnished. Is it going too far? Do I really have a choice?

I kind of hint around with Trudy. She knows where I am going, and she has to grant written approval in order for me to do it: I just can't walk into an endocrinologist's office and say, "Hey! Got any estrogen for me today?" Trudy gets up out of her chair. She walks around the office, and I can tell she, too, is wondering if it is the right thing to do. She knows more about me than any person in the world. Every secret and desire and fantasy. She knows I have children. She knows that giving up Bruce carries with it enormous implications. She knows all these things. Which makes her conclusion all the more important.

You know what? I think it would be good for you.

Trudy calls an endocrinologist she knows in Beverly Hills and tells him the circumstances and the need for total discretion. I speak to him on the phone. He is reading a book on Russian history at the time and says he is going to give me a code name from the book. I don't remember the name now, although I know it wasn't Igor. That way when I call the secretary and give my code name, he will know who it is and take the call. As a further precaution I go after hours when no one is in the office on Wilshire Boulevard besides him. He puts me on a regimen of shots. I also take a testosterone blocker in pill form.

I feel my emotional state changing with hormone therapy. The estrogen begins to have a calming effect after just a few months. Before I had an edge. I could be snappy and irritable. Estrogen takes the edge off. I don't seem to be so uptight about everything—my identity, my gender, the daily tasks of life that annoy me when they should not. Three months into therapy I find myself lying in bed at the Malibu shack crying my eyes out at some melodramatic movie on television.

My God, what the hell are you crying over? What's wrong with you?

I have never done that before, nothing even close. I learn a lesson—I will never ever say to a woman, *Why are you crying over this?* when we go to the movies.

Okay, girls, I get it.

All of this is still not enough. I need to venture out even more. I am still worried about getting caught. But the possibility only heightens the risk. How much can I get away with? The risk is not the foundation of why I am changing my appearance. But given I am basically living my life as a hermit in the Malibu shack, I need some excitement somewhere. I push the envelope even more. I know I am playing with fire.

I am about to get terribly burned.

—✣—

Chapter Eight

Busted

Maybe I am getting careless. Maybe I am getting bold. Most likely I just don't want the role of Bruce anymore since I have decided to transition. The woman inside me has always been clawing and scratching to get out. Bruce cannot handle her. Bruce does not want to handle her. Bruce wants to have simply not existed in the first place. He never belonged. He has worn out his welcome. Here's your medal back.

Obviously when you have a nose job of sorts and your beard removed and the effects of hormones kick in, people are going to notice. I don't think anybody suspects that I am in the actual process of transitioning, but they do think I am looking stranger than ever these days. My upping the ante only adds to the rumors that Bruce Jenner is off his rocker. Maybe they do think I am becoming a woman. But so be it. Nothing matters. I am depressed, and I am not someone prone to depression. My loneliness is so powerful I can taste it as I wake up in the morning to another day of indifference.

It is hard to know what I would do without Wendy Roth. She continues to be a remarkable friend, allowing me to pour out my soul. Jayne Modean, an actress and model, is someone else I confide in. Then there is Tomisu Friedkin, a vintage Texas girl from a vintage Texas family of wealth and grand style. The first name alone is a dead giveaway.

I meet Tomisu while giving a speech in Houston. Breasts are definitely beginning to show, but Tomisu either doesn't notice or doesn't care. I do have them well hidden, and they are always less visible when I'm wearing a suit.

I notice her right away because of the great outfit she has on—a flowing gray dress—and I immediately admire her style and wish I could wear the same. We exchange numbers, and see each other again. She invites me to the ranch her parents own in Colorado. I stay there several days, and it is one of the few instances, maybe the only one, where I distinctly remember having a good time in the mid to late 1980s.

We fish and ride horses. Tomisu and her dad, Tom, want me to go hunting with them, not terribly surprising since as soon as you walk into the main house there is a stuffed polar bear on its hind legs that looks about twelve feet high. There are other trophies of animals on the wall, so it's clear that Tom Friedkin is a big-game hunter. So is

Tomisu, for that matter; she once sent me a picture of her standing next to a lion.

I like to accommodate. I don't like hunting at all, but they work on me and sort of convince me that killing animals such as deer or elk is good because it controls the size of the herd and prevents overpopulation and starvation. Tom is particularly persuasive.

Dammit, you are helping nature if you go out there and get one of these things.

We set out on horseback. We go down a road and scan with our binoculars when we see a deer with a large rack of antlers. Tomisu whispers instructions.

Okay, get off the horse.

I get off the horse.

Like I say, I do what I am told.

I can see the deer thirty or forty yards away through the scope of the rifle they have given me. I'm looking at the trigger, and then back at the deer and then back at the trigger.

My finger is on the trigger now. I don't know if I want to pull it or not, but I am surrounded by hunters and when in Rome...

I'm about to squeeze the trigger.

I can't back down now. I have to take the shot.

I squeeze the trigger.

There is a loud boom. The deer disappears into the woods.

I missed.

Thank God.

I actually missed on purpose by raising the barrel up a little bit before I shot. I may want to kill Bruce, but I am not going to kill an innocent animal.

I do my best to act as if I am disappointed, that I was really looking forward to taking the deer home with me to Malibu and mounting it on the wall of the shack to give it a little added color next to the couch and chairs.

Damn, I missed!

Tomisu and I continue to be close friends for a year. I love being with her, and she loves being with me. There is chemistry. But my sense is she is looking for a full-blown romantic relationship, and I don't want that, nor do I think I am capable of it. I don't want to hurt her or think I am rejecting her, so I tell her the truth and confide in her about my gender dysphoria. She takes it well and does not seem shocked or turned off.

I don't know if she is thinking of marriage, but it is my habit when I find a single woman I instinctively feel close to. I have tried marriage twice, and I have failed both times. I don't want to put myself through that again, and I don't want to put her or anyone else through it.

I am too far down the road of transitioning anyway, and I am not turning back. I am only going deeper.

I have a friend named Bob Flaherty who does traffic reports in Los Angeles, and we have flown together and like each other. He wants me to do an interview for a fundraiser. The day before I had a round of electrolysis with Olga. She has done my chin, and the next day when

I wake up it is red and swollen. It looks like I went three rounds with the woman inside me.

I can't go to that thing today. There's no way. I need to get ice on it.

But Flaherty has been good to me, so I can't suddenly bail out. I do what I always do, come armed with the excuse in case my swollen chin comes up—I banged it on something. Fortunately no one brings it up, although it does look pretty nasty.

Wigs are still hit and miss. I still don't dare do it in person until I realize Halloween is coming up.

Halloween! The best day of the year!

I walk into one of those Halloween costume stores and tell them I want to dress as a woman. They think that's hilarious and give me a wig to wear that I can actually try on in person.

I'm driving on Santa Monica Boulevard later that night and am at a stoplight when my next-door neighbor recognizes my car and pulls up next to me. I can tell he is surprised.

Oh my God, what are you doing!?

I'm going to a Halloween party!

Oh, okay! Have fun!

It is a close call, but I think I have gotten away with it. Actually I am not sure. But I do make a mental note to never drive my Porsche again when I am in women's clothing. It's too easy for somebody to notice a fancy car.

I am a factory race car driver at the time for Ford

Motor Company. They have given me a Mustang to drive around town, and I think to myself that this is the perfect stealth car since nobody knows I even have it. Just in case, I keep a change of clothing in the backseat so I can quickly switch if something unexpected happens. It is more of a security blanket than anything else, since changing clothes in a Mustang when you are six-foot-two is not easy. I also have a pack of makeup remover wipes.

I worry about getting stopped by the police, so I always check to make sure all the car lights are working beforehand and go the speed limit. I am on the Pacific Coast Highway one night in the slow lane to the right. Suddenly I see in my rearview mirror the headlights of a car coming up. It must be doing eighty to ninety miles an hour, and I have no time to react. He shoots the gap between my vehicle and some cars in the parking lane all the way to the right. He hits a parked vehicle, bounces off it, and then goes back onto the highway and keeps flying. Then I see another car chasing him down the center lane.

I miss getting into an accident by several inches. But what goes through my mind is not the severity of any injury I might have sustained but the likelihood of getting caught. An accident would mean the police, which would mean potentially a lot of explaining to do once I gave them my driver's license and they saw the name Bruce Jenner. I obviously am not breaking any law. I can dress however I want. But once the cop saw my driver's license, he would think it was strange, very strange. He

174

would undoubtedly tell other cops, who would tell other people, and it would only be a matter of time before the tabloids got it.

As a last-gasp measure I start carrying in my glove compartment a letter from Trudy Hill saying that I am gender dysphoric and am in therapy and part of the therapy is to drive around dressed as a woman. It probably will not do a bit of good, but I am still trying to cover my tracks.

Driving around is liberating to a certain degree. But it also heightens my isolation. I can't just drive around for the rest of my life. I need to at least find a place where I can get dressed and walk around a little bit. But I can't be stupid like I was in the early 1980s when I drove from Malibu to LAX. I had no plane to catch: I just wanted to park the car and walk along the strip of sidewalk outside one of the terminals. It is always in shadow, so I felt safe: the lights inside were way too bright. I walked up and down for a little bit and then went back to the parking lot. Makeup and wigs were still quite foreign to me then.

As I neared my car another vehicle passed me with the windows down. I heard a voice from inside:

Hey, that's Bruce Jenner!

I beat it out of there. Fortunately I didn't have very far to go. I jumped in my car and drove away as fast as I could and just hoped the driver of the other vehicle didn't come back around for another look. Luckily he did not.

I was pissed at myself afterward for getting recognized.

I also lost confidence and realized that if I was going to keep doing this, I had to get better at it—I couldn't wear a short dress because it attracted too much attention, I had to improve applying makeup, I had to do a more thorough job of plucking my eyebrows.

And yet once again I couldn't deny the exhilaration of it all, the excitement and feeling of being right on the edge in a life that is devoid of either. I knew I was risking everything—my job, my reputation, all my relationships. Maybe in some subconscious way I wanted to get discovered because then, once the media frenzy was over, it would be easier to transition. But the experience at LAX showed I wasn't ready. Once that exhilaration faded, I felt out of breath as I drove back home to Malibu afterward. Sometimes you can feel terrified in a good way. But I felt plain terrified, and it took me a long time after that to get up the courage to venture out again.

Transitioning for me was like standing on a cliff with the beautiful turquoise of the ocean down below. All I had to do was jump to feel the freedom of that water rushing around me. I knew the feeling of it would be unlike anything I had ever experienced before. I so welcomed that. *Take the plunge. Just take it and set yourself free.* But whenever I got too close I took a step back.

Removing the beard I could get away with. The nose job I could get away with. The development of breasts from the hormones?

Not so easy.

I always wear something tight underneath to bind them and then a baggy shirt. Unless it's a suit. But one time I am a guest on Dick Van Patten's parody instructional video *Dirty Tennis*. In the show Van Patten, who is an excellent tennis player, shows ways in which to cheat that are ludicrous. The show is fun and goofy and I like that. The producers pick out a shirt for me to wear. It is too tight. The actress Nicolette Sheridan is also a guest on the show. We appear together and, for whatever reason, she puts her hand on my shirt. She is clearly startled. She feels something she did not expect.

Oh my God! What are those?! They're bigger than mine!

I don't miss a beat and keep right on trucking. Nobody says anything else.

Another escape.

Getting mic'd up for television is also tricky. Normally the sound person goes underneath your shirt to pull the microphone up. That's not happening.

I know I am really playing with fire at this point. I also know I have to take these risks in order to survive. It's okay when I basically lock myself in my house and never leave. No fear of detection there. I can dress to my heart's content. But despite my reclusiveness I still have to deal with the outside world. To generate income I keep doing the speeches even though I feel like a fraud—Future Farmers of America in Kansas City, the American Diabetes Association, the emcee of the Eagle Scout banquet of the Boy Scouts of America. You name it, over the years I have probably been there. I am also doing the usual corporate work, which accounts for about 80 percent of my speaking business—such companies as IBM and Merck. I primarily speak to sales forces, revving them up with my rah-rah pitch. The money is anywhere from $15,000 to $25,000, which is why I always say that Jesse James should have gone into the speaking business rather than robbing banks.

It also means a lot of people are seeing me. Which of course gears up the rumor mill.

By the mid to late 1980s I am also venturing into what passes for downtown Malibu. I go a few times when it's daylight out. I wear hats or sunglasses or both to conceal Bruce. But the sun is too bright and there is no place to hide in shadow. So I start going only at night. I think I am safe, but looking back, I am now sure I was recognized.

The rumors aren't mere rumors anymore. As best as I can remember there are several small items in the tabloids. Then I learn that the *New York Times* has been poking around wondering what the hell is going on with me and seeing if they can pin down a story that I am a cross-dresser.

I cannot keep silent now. I have to tell the triumvi-rate that oversees my career: my manager, George Wallach; Alan Nierob of the public relations firm Rogers and Cowan; my lawyer, Alan Rothenberg.

I am giving a speech in Colorado Springs, Colorado, and I fly there in the Baron with George. I do the event and then we fly back. I am in the left seat piloting, and he is in the right seat. We are flying above the Rockies at an altitude of 22,000 feet. It is an excellent place to talk to someone, a ready-made captive audience. George isn't going anywhere, and neither am I.

I try to bring it up as matter-of-factly as I can:

George, there are some things I gotta talk to you about.

He has obviously noticed changes in my appearance, but he is shocked when I tell him I am seriously thinking of transitioning before I am forty. In the case of George, there is a practical reason I need to speak to him—we have to figure out a way to kill that potential story in the *Times*. I still worry about the impact on my children. I still need an income.

The job falls to Nierob, and there is no one better.

He pounds the crap out of the *Times*.

It works.

But I realize more than ever the repercussions of potential discovery, and not only because of the kids and making a living. I have had a chance to see how people close to me react, which is not to react at all. After those meetings with the triumvirate, my gender issues are never mentioned again. I guess they don't know what to say, or are afraid of saying something wrong, or assume I don't want to talk about it anymore, when the opposite is true. I want to talk about it with the handful of people I trust. I have spent so much of my life not talking about it. When they don't, I wonder if they view me differently, which in turn makes me think I never should have told them.

Down the road, somewhere around 2013, I will talk to Kim about all my issues before any of the other kids. Of all the Kardashians, she is the easiest to talk to and the most empathetic. Now that I have transitioned I hear from her regularly.

Several years before transition she will catch me in the garage wearing women's clothing. Whatever explanation I will give, and I don't exactly remember, it will be lousy. But she doesn't bring it up. By 2013 there will be stories about my desire to transition to a woman regularly in the tabloids. So she will come up to me one day in the house where Kris and I will still be living in Hidden Hills.

What the heck is going on with you?

I will still be so reluctant to tell any of the kids. Part of me will also be dying to talk about it to someone in my family.

You name the day. I'll come over to your house, where it's quiet and nobody else is around.

I will sit with Kim in her living room and tell her what is going on inside and the issues that have been with me all my life. She will mostly listen. I will try to be gentle about it like I had been with George Wallach. She will be opening up some boxes of clothing in the kitchen, and as I am leaving I can't resist.

Anything in there for me?

She will laugh and I will laugh and we will hug. It will feel extraordinary to get this off my chest with a family member. I will feel the path has been opened with her for

With my son Brandon in 1981. I wasn't nearly as present with the children from my first two marriages as I should have been. I felt unworthy as a father and not good enough to play a role in anyone's life. For long periods of time I shamefully abandoned them. *(Original print courtesy of the Jenner family)*

Commentating a sporting event for NBC in 1985. Broadcasting seemed like a natural fit on the surface, but I hated reading from the teleprompter because of my dyslexia. (l-r: Charlie Jones, my son Brandon, Bruce, and Ahmad Rashad) *(David Madison/Getty Images)*

At an event in 1986 pictured with race car driver Danny Sullivan (left) and actor James Garner (right). The afterglow of the Olympics had largely faded by the mid-1980s. I did some events here and there but didn't have any real motivation. I became totally fixated on my gender identity and lived as a hermit much of the time. *(David McGough/Getty Images)*

At an event in 1987 with pioneer transgender activist Renée Richards. I so admired her efforts and envied her courage, but didn't have the nerve to talk to her about my gender issues. *(Ron Galella/Getty Images)*

After a courtship of just 7 months, Kris and I were married in 1991. Regardless of the differences that developed in our relationship later on, she did save me, just like sports saved me as a young child. (l-r: Esther, Robert, Kourtney, Burt, Bill, Kim, Bruce, Brandon, Kris, Casey, Harry Shannon, Brody, Mary Jo Shannon, Khloe) *(Photo Courtesy of Wendy Roth)*

The 1993 Jenner–Kardashian leather-clad family portrait for the annual Christmas card. We were truly one big happy family in the early 1990s. It was the first time I felt like a *real* and present father. But as the years progressed, the complexities of divorce and other issues made it impossible to keep the two families together. (back row l-r: Burt, Khloe, Bruce, and Kris; middle row: Robert, Casey, and Kim; front row l-r: Kourtney, Brody, and Brandon) *(Donaldson Collection/Getty Images)*

Promoting season 1 of *Keeping Up with the Kardashians* in 2007. Once the show took off, my marriage with Kris radically changed, and I no longer felt needed. What kept me going was being a father to the Kardashian kids and Kendall and Kylie. (l-r: Ryan Seacrest, Kim, Kylie, Khloe, Kendall, Kourtney, Kris, and Bruce) *(Jeff Vespa/Getty Images)*

At a celebrity golfing event in 2008. I have always loved playing golf. As Bruce I preferred to play alone, almost as a form of therapy to give me some peace away from the constantly chaotic comings and goings of the Kardashian household. *(John M. Heller/Getty Images)*

The Jenner family in 2011. They have what their father never had: They know who they are and they are comfortable with who they are. (l-r: Burt, Kendall, Kylie, Bruce, Brody, Casey, and Brandon) *(Original print courtesy of the Jenner family)*

At an event in 2012 holding the Wheaties box. For years I would do "Finding the Champion Within" speaking events all over the country. It was my job but also an opportunity to go to hotels and get fully dressed as the woman inside me. *(Noel Vasquez/ Getty Images)*

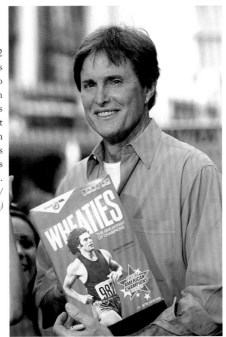

My first public appearance as Caitlyn was at the ESPYs Awards in July 2015. Here I am right before I accept the Arthur Ashe Award for Courage, just hoping I don't trip when I take the stairs to the stage. Next to me are the two women who have been the most influential in my life: my mom, Esther, and my sister, Pam. *(Kevin Mazur/Getty Images)*

Here I am after the ESPYs ceremony with my children who have all been so incredibly supportive. (back row l-r: Khloe, Kim, Kendall, Me, Casey, Kylie, Kourtney, Kaitlynn Carter, and Val Pitalo; front row l-r: Burt, Brandon, Brody, and Michael Marino) *(Courtesy of Caitlyn Jenner)*

On tour with my amazing *I Am Cait* sisters. They have inspired me and taught me so much about the issues facing the transgender community. (l-r: Chandi Moore, Candis Cayne, me, Ella Giselle, Jenny Boylan, and executive producer Andrea Metz) *(Frederick M. Brown/Stringer/Getty Images)*

With Kris at an event in 2016. We have been through a lot over the years, but we will forever share in common our love for the kids and will always be there for them. *(Dimitrios Kamouris/ Getty Images)*

At the *Sports Illustrated* cover shoot at the University of Oregon, where I set a world record in the decathlon. It was strange to be back with photographer Heinz Kluetmeier 40 years after he captured my Olympic win. While Bruce will forever be stuck in that moment, Caitlyn never was and never will be. *(Courtesy of Caitlyn Jenner)*

At a LGPA pro-am golfing event in 2016. Unlike Bruce, I now love golfing with others. Plus my short game has improved. *(Ryan Young/Getty Images)*

With a fully restored 1960 Sprite, the same model of car that my dad had when I was a kid. On the back it says "Dad's Sprite," a tribute I know he would have loved. I will never know how my father would have reacted to Caitlyn, but he would have wanted me to be happy. I think about him all the time. *(Courtesy of Caitlyn Jenner)*

continued conversation, perhaps acknowledgment of my issues and how I am doing. We talk regularly about almost everything after that but never gender. That bothers me for a long time, that maybe she was not the right person to tell after all. If Kim is uncomfortable, then what about the rest of the world? It is just like Pam's reaction was more than twenty years earlier. The same silence.

From my perspective I am opening up the golden gate of gender and want Kim to walk through it with me. I even have the idea that we might go shopping together.

Several years later I ask her: *How come I never heard from you?*

I just didn't know what to do, if I should talk about it.

After she says that I understand completely. I am not a distant cousin or uncle. I am Kim's stepfather telling her that I have this relentless urge to look like her stepmother. As for Pam, I was her famous baby brother who she had witnessed winning the decathlon in Montreal. Their silence did hurt me, but I now realize my expectations were unreasonable.

I am now almost forty. I feel good about all the things I have done, allowed the woman inside me to live and breathe when she can't be suffocated anyway.

I am about to take the final step.

Until...

I still care about what people think of me. Becoming a trans woman is about a million miles away from the image that many more millions still have of Bruce Jenner. As helpful as Trudy Hill has been, I feel there is still so much I don't understand. I have never knowingly talked to a trans woman. The only trans person I know of is Renée Richards, who made headlines around the world in 1977 when she petitioned and won the right to play in the US Open tennis tournament as a woman after transitioning. I met her once at a banquet. I admired and envied her, but I didn't have the courage to speak to her of my own gender issues.

And what about my four kids, who range in age from six to eleven? They have the same image of their father as the rest of the world. How would they possibly handle my transition, given the era? How comfortable would my first two wives be with me seeing the kids? They would never openly deny me, but I get the feeling sometimes that they would think it might be better if the contact was limited. I would understand their hesitation: it would be traumatizing for any child to try to understand that their dad is now a woman. Linda says I told her at one point that I was seriously thinking of having surgery overseas and coming back as a close female relative, an aunt or something. I don't remember ever saying that, and I had absolutely no intention of doing so. But I can see why I might have said it, a desperate way of lessening the shock for my kids.

If I become a woman, I will be my real self. That would be sublime, but I also have to face reality. Bruce still has earning potential. Bruce pays the bills. Bruce is tired of being lonely and isolated and wonders if as a trans woman she would be even more lonely and isolated.

So I stop going through transition in 1989.

I can't do this to my kids.

I can't do this to me.

I can't do this to society. It is not ready.

I have to get back in the game. I have to once again establish Bruce as the dominant presence, no matter how much I loathe him. I need cover again, and the best way to find cover, because of the rumors still engulfing me, is to start dating again.

Which is when Kris Kardashian and Bruce Jenner improbably find each other.

—⁓—

December 20, 2015

"It's a movie..."

I am at the movies in Westlake.

I realize now I should not have gone. I should have checked with activists in the trans community to make sure the movie had their seal of approval. I should have been more sensitive that when you are in the public eye, you are held up as a symbol and spokesperson for something whether you like it or not. Everything you do will be under scrutiny.

But in my mind it was still harmless.

It was a movie.

The transgender community is a rainbow of many opinions. Many, many opinions. I love that. I respect that. I have strong opinions myself, and I don't assume everyone will agree. I expect to be condemned by such groups as the religious right. I did not expect some members of the transgender community would find fault with me as well, sometimes viciously.

The film in question is *The Danish Girl*, starring Eddie Redmayne. It is based on the life of Lili Elbe, the first trans woman to undergo gender-affirming surgery in 1930. She died of complications roughly a year later.

I watched the film with obvious interest, both from historical and personal perspectives. As I watched, I continued to wonder if I should have the Final Surgery or not. I thought Redmayne was incredible, just as he was as Stephen Hawking in *The Theory of Everything*, a role for which he won an Academy Award for best actor.

Certain members of the trans community detested the film because they resented a cis man (a person having the identity they were assigned at birth) playing Elbe and thought a transgender person should have been given the role—valid criticism and concern. They felt the film was laden with stereotypes, showed lack of care and respect for trans women, and was what the blogger Sally Jane Black called "facile, narrow-minded, misguided-at-best trash."

And those were her positive points.

Many, as it turned out, shared the same viewpoint that it was a rotten film that never should have been made.

I, on the other hand, assumed the film took creative license. After all, it is not a documentary and the purpose was to create something eye-opening and entertaining for a global audience.

In other words, an enjoyable two hours, and that was pretty much that.

Or so I thought.

Prior to the release of the film Redmayne made a major mistake: in an interview with *Out* magazine, he said he saluted my courage. I took it as a compliment at the time. It sounded like a compliment. It actually was a compliment.

Right?

Wrong...

Based on Redmayne's remark there were a spate of stories in the British press that Redmayne and I had arranged to meet at the Academy Awards. Which naturally created another rumor that I had *already* met with Redmayne to praise his performance in the film. This infuriated members of the trans community because it led them to believe I was publicly endorsing the film even though I had never met with Redmayne or had any specific plan to do so.

Nick Adams, director of programs, transgender media for GLAAD, who has been an incredible resource in guiding me through the thicket, alerted me. I also received a flurry of text messages from fellow *I Am Cait* sister Jenny Boylan, a highly respected member of the trans community and the Anna Quindlen Writer-in-Residence at Barnard College who wrote a marvelous book on her transition called *She's Not There: A Life in Two Genders*. She is my consigliere on gauging the mood of the community, and it just might be a full-time job at this point.

(Note: the following exchange did actually happen word-for-word.)

> JENNY: I just wanted to whisper in your ear that if you did meet with [Redmayne] a lotta trans people would be all mad because *Danish Girl* is

problematic. You can and should of course do as you like. But I do try to protect you from unnecessary turmoil when I can.

CAITLYN: Why is the community up in arms about Eddie? I saw the film and it was great.

JENNY: It's very complicated.

CAITLYN: Briefly try to explain.

JENNY: But the film is not accurate. It's a Hollywood/adapted version of a fictionalized version of a story of a trans woman from eighty years ago. It's not an accurate story. It suggests that forced feminization and clothing are what triggers the transgender impulse. When we all know it goes much deeper. Also...

CAITLYN: You're right, it's a movie. And it has to be entertaining. I thought it was very well done.

JENNY: The community is very tired of cisgender actors playing us and getting credit for being so brave when it's our actual lives that are being portrayed. I thought the movie was beautiful in places, and that Eddie was really interesting to watch.

CAITLYN: Please, community, get a life. He was great and deserves an Oscar.

JENNY: Well, maybe so. But if you publicly endorse the film or him I assure you that you will have a firestorm on your hands again...are you meeting with Eddie?

CAITLYN: Okay, I got it!

JENNY: All I really care about is keeping you from getting hurt.

CAITLYN: Nobody's going to hurt me. They don't like me or anybody who's in the public eye. It's sad.

JENNY: Eddie is a great actor. But the part that he is playing is a cisgender actor's portrayal of a cisgender screenwriter's adaptation of a cisgender novelist's fictionalized version of a transgender person's life. It's kind of like if you watched *Star Wars* in hopes of learning a whole lot about science. Does this make any sense?

CAITLYN: No, and these people don't make any sense.

I was sincerely thankful to Jenny for the heads-up. I know she was just trying to protect me, and I did hear their criticisms loud and clear. The trans community has been through so much that there is no such thing as overreaction. Which doesn't mean I necessarily agree with it all the time.

Upon further reflection and review, I now have this to say about *The Danish Girl* and Eddie Redmayne's performance:

Privately, I thought the film was marvelously entertaining, and Redmayne's performance deserved an Oscar. While trans women and trans men *must* be better represented in Hollywood (like African Americans and members of the gay and lesbian community and women and everyone else who is not a white male), I can't imagine anyone who could have played the role better than he did.

But publicly, when I went to the *Vanity Fair* Oscar party in February 2016, these were my thoughts: *Please, Eddie, do not make any eye contact or God forbid smile or, worst of all, come up to me to talk. Turn your back, or head in the opposite direction, or just leave. I am also putting you on notice that if asked about the film, I will say it was shameful.*

Sound ridiculous?

Of course it does, because it is ridiculous. *The Danish Girl* is not perfect in terms of approaching the subject matter. But we as a community should be excited about the film because it brings attention and exposure to the struggle that all trans people face regardless of who we are and where we come from and how much money we have or don't have. I wanted to talk about the film. What resonated for me was the pain Elbe went through because of an intolerant and hateful society. That has tremendous application today for a public that so often refuses to understand. Compassion leads to not only acceptance but the joy of acceptance, so it isn't mere obligation. And yes, I wanted to meet Eddie Redmayne. But not after being told by someone who only has my best interests at heart that it would cause members of the trans community to become upset with me. So I had no choice then but to be silent.

It becomes frustrating and debilitating and depressing to have to censor yourself like this. For a community pushing for acceptance, we can sadly be brutally judgmental of each other. We insist upon tolerance, but only to an extent. We want inclusion, but aren't as inclusive at times. We want to stamp out hate, and yet there are members of the trans community who take great pleasure and satisfaction in expressing their hate for me when all I have tried to do is ceaselessly advocate for my sisters and brothers. We publicly argue against stereotypes, and yet I am repeatedly condemned for not being a stereotypical trans woman.

Don't get me wrong, I have received many positive comments from the trans community. Institutions such as GLAAD have been fantastically supportive. So has the mainstream public, with the exception of anonymous cowardly commenters on the Internet.

I realize I can't please everybody. All I can do is be myself, and it's taken me sixty-five years to do that. I have had a steep learning curve in a short amount of time. But those who criticize me only know what they read. And this is not a fair representation of who I am. I also think many people make the assumption that because I was on *Keeping Up with the Kardashians*, I am as frivolous as the show is often meant to be. But I am not that way in real life.

From the very beginning of when I decided to transition, I made a conscious effort to limit my exposure in the mainstream media (the tabloids make up whatever they want), because I didn't want to be seen everywhere. I am very selective when it comes to interviews with the mainstream media. I have said yes to maybe a dozen out of hundreds of requests. One of the criteria is that the needs of the trans community be addressed in any interview with more than obligatory lip service.

But how can we expect people on the outside to support and push for us when we fight among ourselves? We have to support each other's differences, agree more, listen to each other (including me), and sacrifice smaller fights and disagreements for bigger advances and gains. United we will succeed. Divided we never will.

Because of the attention I received since I transitioned, the word *transgender* has been introduced into the national conversation. I am not solely responsible for this by any stretch. Shows such as *Transparent* and *Orange Is the New Black* have paved the way. So has Janet Mock with her amazing book *Redefining Realness*. So have activists such as Jenny Boylan and Kate Bornstein and many others who are supporters of my cause even though they sometimes blanch at what comes out of my mouth. I do have a big mouth. But I also have a bigger heart.

I have written the following words before, and I am going to write them again and put them in bold for emphasis:

I am white.

I am entitled.

I have wealth.

I know that before I became Caitlyn I lived in a world of white male privilege—exponentially heightened in my case because I was a famous white male athlete. I am aware that I still have that within me. I am also evolving. I am not an arrogant person, and I am certainly not arrogant enough to think that in becoming a woman I suddenly appropriated the institutionalized inferiority with which women have been treated in our society. When women say I have not walked a mile in their shoes, much less a step, they are right. I am not trying to define womanhood.

It is the media that has ordained me the spokesman for the transgender community. Because of the celebrity culture in which we live, I do sometimes draw undue attention. My words are not gospel, even though the media likes to think so. I am very new to the community, and I understand some still perceive me as an outsider. My own story, I believe, is worth telling because the pain and fear I experienced was real, and it is important for the public to understand the ramifications of denying your authentic self.

I have said in the past that "it was easy to come out as trans. It was harder to come out as a Republican." And I understand why some women and men in the trans community cannot understand my choice of party. I readily admit that the GOP platform over the past several decades has been inadequate and disappointing when it comes to LGBTQ issues. I am aware of the spate of anti-LGBTQ bills that have been filed on the state level (more than 175 in 2016, of which forty-four specifically targeted transgender men and women).

Thankfully on the North Carolina bathroom politics issue the US Justice Department filed suit stating that the proposed bathroom law amounts to, as Attorney General Loretta Lynch put it, "state-sponsored discrimination" and "provides no benefit to society." On the same issue, the administration issued a sweeping directive to public schools: transgender students must be allowed access to bathrooms that correspond with their gender identity (now under review by the US Supreme Court). Also in the last year, transgender men and women can now serve openly in the military, and they are on a pathway to receive complete healthcare, inclusive of transition-related medical needs.

I obviously welcome these steps. There must be many more. But I am not a one-issue voter confined solely to LGBTQ issues. I am a conservative, and always have been, particularly on fiscal issues, and I am not going to change to make myself more popular or more politically palatable. I did not transition to become a liberal Democrat.

I believe that we desperately need conservatives like myself who have a platform and can use it to enlighten fellow conservatives, reminding them of the Golden Rule— that trans people should not be judged on moral or religious grounds but rather treated as fellow human beings. Whatever advances we have made, our community is still in dire straits: the shockingly high rates of suicide that show no sign of abatement, the rates of violence and unemployment that are far higher than the general population, and the states making it extremely difficult to change gender markers on official documents such as driver's licenses and birth certificates. The conservative community must be reached to address these critical roadblocks to our equality. I can only reach them by getting them to the table, not by bashing them. Republicans are also in power: the House, the Senate, and the presidency.

I will try as hard as I can to make the government see that lives are at stake. It will be an uphill struggle. I am not starry-eyed. But I do have experience in attaining goals that no one thought possible. I won the decathlon at the Olympics by going after the impossible. I became Caitlyn after saying to myself for sixty-five years that it was impossible. Change comes in the unlikeliest of circumstances unless you give up trying to effect change.

I make a point to answer questions without regard to spin or personal reputation. I swear that my heart is always in the right place, which isn't to say that I am always right. Articulating what I believe is much more important to me than articulating what I want people to think I believe or what people think I should believe. I have been through that already in my life.

During a commercial break after the first taped segment of my *Ellen* appearance in September 2015, Ellen DeGeneres leaned over and, to the best of my recollection, said in a friendly voice:

You know, I heard your views on the marriage equality act and same sex marriage have really progressed over the years.

Yes, they have.

I would love to talk about that.

I believed, as anyone would, that that was exactly what she wanted to talk about—my progression in terms of changing attitude over the years. I said the following when we came back on the air:

Gay marriage. I have to admit that I remember fifteen years ago, twenty years ago, whenever it was, the whole gay marriage issue came up at first, I was not for it. I mean, I thought I am a traditionalist. I'm older than most people in the audience. I mean, I kind of like tradition and it's always between a man and a woman, and I'm thinking I don't quite get it. But as time has gone on, like a lot of people on this issue, I've really changed my thinking here to: I don't ever want to stand in front of anybody's happiness. That's not my job. Okay. If that word *marriage* is really, really that important to you I can go with it.

Ellen responded:

... It's funny you're still kind of a little not on board with it.

I was surprised when she said that. I am for it. I did not initially understand why marriage was so important, influenced no doubt by my own personal experience. Now I do, and it is a wonderful thing to see.

After I appeared on the show, I was publicly accused of being a hypocrite: how can someone in the trans community not be open-minded enough to support the Marriage Equality Act? This discussion only further alienated me from members of the LGTBQ community. Ellen's appearance on *The Howard Stern Show*, where in my mind she even more emphatically took what I said out of context, made it go viral.

Several months later, in a lengthy interview in *Time*

magazine in December 2015 after being on the short list for Person of the Year, I was asked a question about image. I gave the following reply:

> One thing that has always been important to me, and it may seem very self-absorbed or whatever, is first of all your presentation of who you are. I think it's much easier for a trans woman or a trans man who authentically kind of looks and plays the role. So what I call my presentation I try to take that seriously. I think it puts people at ease. If you're out there and, to be honest with you, if you look like a man in a dress, it makes people uncomfortable.

Not a great career move...

I have examined what I said in *Time*. I have thought about it. But I won't disavow it. A trans woman who looks like a man in a dress makes people uncomfortable: just watch the look on their faces when they see one, or how they instantly look away. Any man wearing a dress for whatever reason makes them uncomfortable. Any man who wears nail polish makes them uncomfortable. Anyone who is gender fluid makes them uncomfortable. The majority of the public is made uncomfortable by anything that isn't mainstream. It is a commentary on them and not the other way around. But we cannot ignore it.

What I am trying to do, what I am doing, is to ultimately make the mainstream public comfortable with us, or at least semi-comfortable, since changing attitudes may be the hardest societal task of all. The best way for me to do that right now is to meet people and show them I am friendly and "normal," because I am friendly and "normal" to the degree that anyone is normal. Like every other trans person I have met. I want to be accessible.

Am I engaging in some superficial notion of womanhood because I want to look as good as I can? Actually the reason is simpler than that:

I like to look good. It is important to me. I am not trying to make any judgment on womanhood as it applies to physical characteristics. I have absolutely no right to do that. I also know that I have the money for surgeries, a luxury that most trans women do not have. For me, it boils down to the fact that some women and some men are consumed with the way they look, and some just care the usual amount, and some don't care at all. It is a trait of personality, and everyone is different.

All the criticisms sting, but I brush them away. I will continue to push issues facing the transgender community in the best way I see fit, disregarding those who attack me for the advancement of their own agenda or to be inflammatory in the inflammatory age in which we live.

But I have learned some lessons.

The next time Eddie Redmayne plays a trans woman, count me out.

—◆—

Chapter Nine

Here's Brucie!!

The first time I hear the name Kris Kardashian is in Ketchikan, where all I just want to do is catch a fish.

I am in Alaska in 1990 with former Los Angeles Dodgers and San Diego Padres first baseman Steve Garvey and his wife, Candace, shooting a television show in which we are salmon fishing. I have known Garvey for a long time—the fraternity of sports celebrities is smaller and tighter than Yale's Skull and Bones—and the arc of his public life has been eerily similar to mine. When he was with the Dodgers and Padres, he was known as Mr. Clean. He played through whatever it took for 1,207 straight games, still the National League record. His sturdy solid-jaw looks were referred to over and over again. He inherited the crown of the All-American sports hero after I lost it because of my messy personal life and controversial divorces. The press went over the top in depicting him just like they did me. *Sports Illustrated* wrote:

For most of his 41 years Garvey lived at the corner of Straight and Narrow. He played football at Michigan State. Graduated with a B average. Signed with his boyhood idols, the Dodgers. Married the prettiest girl in school and had two daughters Norman Rockwell might have painted...

Sound familiar? It sure did to me. From my own experience I knew there was only one way for Garvey to go, and that was down into the pits. Garvey's messy personal life, culminating in a horrible divorce from his first wife, Cyndy, in 1983 that went public and a child born out of wedlock after an affair, turned Mr. Clean filthy. He had done what he had done. But it was the glee and venom and mockery with which he was dismantled that I so identified with, built up by the media out of all proportion and then crucified for it exactly as it was for me. The only thing worse than being called Mr. Clean is the Golden Boy. Or Prince Valiant. Or Adonis...

It's probably why we are fishing together in Alaska, the ultimate hideout where not even the bears read the tabloids.

I am wearing sweat pants, attire I think appropriate for fishing. Maybe I look a little slovenly for television, but I have never been a clotheshorse. As far back as I can remember it was the women in my life, starting with my mother, who bought all my clothing, with the exception of that pair of tight bell-bottoms in college. My lack of style is such that *GQ*, a magazine dedicated to style, has gone out of its way to point out that I have none.

Candace shows up in her customary outfit of head-to-toe Ralph Lauren. She looks like she is just off the runway, not the kind of person interested in bait on the hook. She takes one look at me and decides this will not do at all, probably because she is right: I look even more of a wreck than usual because I am a wreck, trying to put together the pieces of my life and not really knowing if I will be able to.

Candace thinks I need a woman:

I have a friend who would be perfect for you.

Who is it?

Her name is Kris Kardashian. She is in the process of a divorce and lives in Beverly Hills.

Beverly Hills? Way out of my league. I'm not interested.

Steve, what do you think about Bruce and Kris going out together?

It'll never work.

Now I am interested. As much as I love Garvey, I generally try to do the opposite of anything he says. There is a reserve that just makes you to want to go up to him and muss up his hair and watch as he uses a slide rule to put it back in place. But there is still hesitation on my part.

Chrystie and Linda were both down-to-earth, a quality that attracted me to them and was similar to myself. A woman from Beverly Hills strikes me as the very opposite, most days spent shopping in the fashionable boutiques and brand-name stores that rim Rodeo Drive. Kris is also in the process of a divorce, and the last thing I need is somebody coming out of a divorce, given my own track record.

Candace now tends to agree.

She has four children. It would never work.

The wheels click in my mind:

She has four children.

I have four children.

That's eight kids.

Kris has the same amount of baggage that I do.

Now I really am interested.

Candace quickly sets something up for the following week. Garvey and I are playing in Magic Johnson's golf tournament at the Riviera Country Club, the historic course in Pacific Palisades. She invites Kris to join us at a party afterward and then dinner.

Kris brings along her nanny, which is open to many interpretations, none of them good.

The first time I see her she is in a white pantsuit. She looks great. I go up to her at the party and put my arms around her.

At last in the arms of a real woman with four children.

I am hoping she will laugh.

She doesn't.

But neither does she look at me like I am crazy. I actually think she is flattered by it or at least thinks it is a step up from *Hey, baby, want to touch my gold medal?*

We mix into the crowd. I know a lot of people there in the way that men know a lot of people, which is to say we don't know anyone at all and float off once the sports talk is exhausted. Kris knows everybody and everybody knows her. They are much more happy to see her than me. I have never met anyone this effortlessly social.

Who is this person?

I still don't know a single thing about her other than the little Candace has told me.

We go out to dinner afterward at Ivy at the Shore in Santa Monica. It is one of those places to be seen, although I prefer to be in places not to be seen and think McDonald's approaches haute cuisine, depending on how crispy the fries are. I have the meatloaf and mashed potatoes because I always have the meatloaf and mashed potatoes when I go out if it's available. Kris knows a lot of people there as well, but once again she doesn't work the room: she really knows these people. It reminds me there is an entire world out there that I knew existed but never felt comfortable with. But I am still not entirely hooked.

Right before we leave Kris applies pencil outliner on her lips. She doesn't even use a mirror. She just goes *zip zip zip*. It's perfect. Now, I actually know something about using pencil outliner, and it's very hard to do without a mirror (although I am proud to say I have mastered it).

Now I'm hooked. A year ago, even six months ago, that simple act would have heightened my gender issues. I would have felt the familiar pang of envy that she can simply do this whenever she wants wherever she wants. She doesn't carry a pack of makeup remover wipes in case the police stop her. She doesn't carry around a note from the therapist. She hasn't thought about gender a single minute in her life. Why would she? Why would anyone I know? It's not an issue. But now that I have decided not to transition, I am trying not to make it an issue as well, suppress my urges to the greatest extent possible. I cannot afford them in my life anymore. I don't want them.

Kris and I start going out. I have a dinner scheduled one night with a producer acquaintance I know and bring Kris along. Since he is in the business it is one of his job requirements to act as if he knows everyone in the business. He is showing off a little bit, another job requirement, self-importance as a work of art. But every time he mentions someone, Kris says she not only knows her or him but also the entire family, without trying to show off in the least. Finally flummoxed, the producer turns to her in the middle of dinner and says:

Who are you?

To which Kris says something so uncharacteristic of her today that it seems hard to believe she said it, but she did, because I was there:

I'm just a mom in Beverly Hills.

Right at that moment I see qualities in Kris that will serve her extraordinarily well and make her *somebody* one day—the way she deals with people and takes charge without them even knowing it, the habit of sending flowers or some other gift after a meeting. A combination of charm and professional intelligence, knowing that remembering a birthday goes a long way because of the attentiveness and thoughtfulness it implies.

She is everything I am not. I am not confident. I am not comfortable in my own skin. I am not social. I am lousy at giving gifts. She is natural and disarming about it all. It doesn't feel remotely like name-dropping when she says she knows this person and that person. It is quiet, sweet really.

I have been in a rat hole the last six years. But I can feel Kris bringing me out of that even after our first few dates. It feels good to go out again after all those years in the Malibu shack.

Whatever the differences that developed between Kris and me later on, and there were big ones at the end, she saved me at this point in my life, just like sports had saved me as a young child.

I fall in love with Kris quickly. She falls in love with me quickly (we marry after a courtship of seven months). Love is at the crux of us. But I believe, and this is my opinion and my opinion only, we both want something from each other.

I know I do.

Kris restores my credibility. She helps to restore the image of Bruce. I also believe, and once again this is my opinion only, that Kris gets something from me. Her divorce from Robert Kardashian, a successful lawyer and entrepreneur later made famous for his ceaseless loyalty to his longtime friend O.J. Simpson when he was tried for murder, had been ugly. Kris had married when she was twenty-two. She told me there was just much more life she wanted to live. She had been involved in an affair with a man in his twenties, which could not have been a boon to the marriage. But close friends of the couple were still shocked when she left. They could not understand why she was willing to give up the Beverly Hills lifestyle. They could not understand how she could cause such tumult to her children. They all loved Robert because there was a great deal to love about Robert—an incredible father, a man of decency who encouraged my role as a stepfather as long as I always remembered that he was the father.

Robert was angry as well. He could not believe that Kris was leaving. There was a great deal of acrimony. As in many difficult divorces, I believe that Robert wanted Kris to realize she had made a terrible mistake and end up in some crappy apartment in the Valley. It didn't happen that way. We made a glamorous couple, clearly in love. We began to have success in business as a team. I was well known. So sometimes I wondered if Kris was making a statement to her former husband: a big fuck you.

Since—let's not kid ourselves—everyone wants to know, Kris and I have good and frequent sex at the beginning. It is imbued with affection and love, but my attitude is no different than it was in high school: I'm just not entirely comfortable with it. Sex, to be sustained in a relationship, requires emotional tools that I simply do not possess because of fear of expressing emotion, to the point where it ultimately became easier to have it only sporadically and then not have it. It means giving, and while I believe I am better now, I have never been good at it.

I tell Kris about my gender issues before I make love to her. I don't want to repeat the unfairness of what I did to Linda, literally springing it on her one day after we had been married for several years. I don't tell her the full extent, that Trudy Hill had said unequivocally that my condition would never change and the only thing I could do was somehow try to live with it on my own terms. But I tell her a great deal.

This will always be a subject of dispute between Kris and me as to how much she could intuit about my gender issues. She insists that she was taken by surprise by my ultimate transition to Caitlyn, which obviously means in her mind that she did not know enough. On *Keeping Up with the Kardashians* she shed copious tears in coming to grips with it. Given what she saw, the whole reaction seemed a little puzzling then and seems puzzling now.

All I know is what I know.

I told her there had been a woman inside me all my life. I told her I dressed as a woman, and she knew I did, because I did it several times in front of her after we were married. I don't know how much I elaborated on the electrolysis to remove the hair from my face and chest, but I would say it was pretty self-evident.

I also told her I had been in hormone therapy for roughly the past four and a half years before stopping six months earlier. It was obvious that the effect of the hormones had caused something—two somethings to be exact. To me they were the development of breasts, size 36B. To Kris they were man boobs caused by my being out of shape. I was out of shape, but not out of shape enough in my mind to cause size 36B man boobs. In my mind, she must have known what they were, which would indicate someone very confused about gender. So, for me, the idea that she was later shocked by my transition is equally shocking to me. It implies that I left her in the dark about the severity of my struggles.

At least to me it does.

Let's leave it at that.

Maybe the fact that we had healthy sex at the beginning, as well as my love of such "macho" activities as skiing and car racing, did indicate to her that my so-called maleness was intact. Maybe she thought that whatever gender issues I had, she could change me.

I did tell Kris I was gender dysphoric. But given my decision roughly a year earlier not to transition, I was determined to never pursue such a path again, applying instead the same willpower and discipline of mind as I had when training for the decathlon. I did not want to ever live my life in seclusion again. I wanted the marriage to work and would do everything to make it work. We did have something going for us: We loved each other, and several years into the marriage had two wonderful children together in Kendall and Kylie. I also love and adore my stepchildren, and I felt the love was mutual as I played a pivotal role in raising them, without ever thinking I was supplanting their father, because I was not.

I wanted this marriage to work. Both of us did until the last five years, when it became acrimonious misery for both of us, a toxic combination of her withering anger with me and my defensiveness and generally being at each other's throats and the kids asking their mother why she yelled at me all the time. We had many great years together beforehand; it only began to implode when *Keeping Up with the Kardashians* became a runaway success and Kris was at the helm of a multimillion-dollar family franchise in which she controlled all the purse strings, including mine.

As we are courting and I see more and more of Kris's personality, it is also clear she can also help me fix my relationship with my kids before it is too late. My connection to Burt and Casey and Brandon and Brody, who are now between eight and thirteen, had never felt right. How could it when I lived with the three boys for at best little more than two years each and never lived with Casey? I like imbuing them with the same sense of adventure that I have—car racing, flying, motocross, activities on the edge. The boys love those activities and will become gifted at them, so something of me rubbed off. I know they were proud of the Jenner name. But my connection to them has never been stable. I know they felt close to me in the late 1980s, but given how much time I had on my hands because I basically wasn't working, I should have seen much more of them.

Linda at one point said to Brandon and Brody that the only thing they need to know about their father is that he lives in an emotional wheelchair. That hurts terribly. But maybe it's true, turning on the switch of disconnect because of my own disconnect.

I do know I love my kids. I do know I want to become a better and more present father. With four kids of her own, Kris knows what it means to be a parent, and she seems to relish juggling eight young lives into the mix.

They all get together for the first time at Kim's tenth birthday party. There is no friction or jealousy, just the common bond of happiness. I sit back and watch and am incredibly moved by what I see. Maybe this can work. Maybe there is a way of making amends.

Not long after that, Kris decides we are going on a ski trip to Deer Valley in Utah. She divides the living room of her Beverly Hills home into eight different piles to make sure each child has the necessary equipment—boots, poles, outfits (no designer required at that point), gloves, hats—and runs out and buys anything that is missing. There are two SUVs just for the luggage to the airport. It is only a family ski trip, albeit a complicated one with a lot of moving parts. But even then you can see Kris take complete charge in the way that will one day make her so successful, figuring out every detail no matter how small, refusing to relax until everything is right in the exact way she wants it right.

Once again I sit back and marvel. Actually, it is much more than that. It is magical that I am here with this woman of vibrancy and style, going skiing with my kids and her kids and everybody having a ball, our true-life version of *Eight Is Enough*.

All the children are there when we get married. Of the thousands of pictures that have been taken of me in my life, one in particular on my wedding day is my favorite. We are on a lawn outside a private home in Beverly Hills. I am sitting in the middle in a black tuxedo and white tie. Brandon is to one side of me and Burt is standing behind him with one hand on Brandon's shoulder and the other holding his hand. Brody is on the other side leaning into me so much that our heads are touching. Casey is sitting in front of me in a white dress with a garland of flowers wrapping around her forehead, blond and lithe and stunningly beautiful. My hand is resting on her forearm. Rob is next to her, looking a little shell-shocked, maybe because he knew something the rest of us did not. Behind Rob is Kim, who even then had the exotic features that will ultimately make her a worldwide sensation. On the other side in a kneeling position is Kourtney, who looks like her sister Kim but with longer hair and lighter features. She is happy and smiling although I know she is struggling with the idea of a stepfather coming into her life. Behind Kourtney is Khloé, standing and impish with a twinkle in her eye and also a touch of the devilish. Kris is in back in a strapless white gown with one arm around Burt and the other around Brandon.

Sometimes pictures lie, particularly wedding pictures. But this one does not. It *was* magical. It *was* a miracle. It *was* truly perfect, or as perfect as anything can be in life. There was no family fame then and no fortune. There was just us.

Kris and I have to figure out how to generate income. I know I need to get back in the game. I am optimistic because I am always optimistic. As much as I struggle with my own issues, I still believe that things will work themselves out. But I have let my career go, and I am not sure at this point to what degree it can be rebuilt. The culture of celebrity does not look kindly upon those who disappear. Becoming relevant again once you have largely made yourself irrelevant is often impossible.

The rumors of my private life don't help, either. Like an infestation of termites they have made their way into the palm tree corridors of Beverly Hills. Even some of Kris's closest friends, at least those who are still talking to her since the divorce from Robert, have heard about them. But Kris vigorously defends me, and after we get married the rumors fade away. Her women friends now love me, and her men friends are probably jealous that I never have to shave.

I am not quite sure where to start in resurrecting my career, but Kris knows exactly. She views it as still one of untapped potential that has been allowed to wilt. All it needs is someone to take control, and Kris will be that someone.

She looks at the team that has been managing me:

Wallach, Rogers and Cowan, and my lawyer, Rothenberg. I am still paying them in one fashion or another, either on retainer or by giving them a percentage of the business I generate, and Kris concludes that they have to go and go quickly, because nothing has happened for quite some time. I come to the same conclusion, but the bonds of loyalty and the hatred of confrontation makes it impossible for me to sever the relationships.

Kris has no such qualms. She doesn't know any of these people. This is business. Purely business.

Why are you paying this guy?

Good question.

How much are you paying this guy?

Better question.

How much has he done for you the last couple of years?

Best question.

We go to George's office. George is on one side of the table, and Kris and I are on the other. Kris does most of the talking.

We're doing this on our own.

George looks at me. I feel compelled to say something:

You did a good job, but we're moving on. We're doing something different.

I feel terrible. I shouldn't, because other than *Grambling's White Tiger*, the television project he brought to me, there has been little in the last eight years as far as I recall. Part of it admittedly is that I didn't want to do anything for some of those years. Kris and I both feel that I need a fresh start. But I feel like I have let him down because of our history. He was my first and best champion.

He came to me before the 1976 Olympics when he saw a preview issue of the Games in *People* with my picture in it. He called directory assistance for San Jose and asked for my number—those were the days your number was listed. He dialed it.

I'm a manager. I would love to talk to you.

He flew to San Jose just to meet with me. Under amateur rules I was not allowed to have a manager before the Games. I told him that.

It's not going to work out, but you never know what the future holds.

I had a good instinct about George. I knew right then and there I would use him if there was any opportunity. He had shown faith in me, unlike all the other managers and agencies who only called me after I was a champion.

He helped sort things out for me the final night of the Games after the closing ceremony when I was naïve about who was who. Like Irwin Weiner, the vice president of financial and talent affairs of ABC and the network's ultimate dealmaker. Everybody knew Irwin, except for me until ten minutes before he approached saying that ABC wanted to hire me. When I excitedly told George, he said it would be best not to commit to anything too quickly since NBC and CBS were keenly interested as well.

It was the beginning of a fun and beautiful relationship,

particularly for the first five or six years when the offers were rolling in and George screened what made sense and what did not. But now the phone isn't ringing off the hook, and it hasn't been ringing off the hook for some time. He is getting 15 percent of my business, which he has certainly been entitled to in the past, but I need to market myself and reinvent myself.

George is shocked. He is looking at Kris, trying to figure out exactly who this woman is and why she has such a hold on me. I know why she has a hold on me: I like strong women, and Kris is the strongest of the strongest.

So *poof*...

That's it for George.

Kris streamlines the business. Ties to Rogers and Cowan are severed. The same with my lawyer. Kris starts making hundreds of calls to corporations extolling my speaking skills because she believes the "Finding the Champion Within" speech is still effective and powerful. She still thinks there are legs in those two days of my life in Montreal. She also sees potential in the licensing of my name on reputable exercise equipment, using as promotion the then ridiculously cheap infomercial at $500 for a half hour. Ultimately we market such products as the Super Step, the Power Trainer, and the Stair Climber Plus. At the peak two thousand infomercials appear a month in seventeen different countries.

On a personal level, Kris gets me back in the gym after

a long absence. I go to Gold's in Venice Beach, and with the exception of those breasts/man boobs (they remain even after stopping hormones), my body begins to build muscle and firm up again. I look good. I feel good.

Sorry to the woman inside me.

Brucie's back in business!

—ɯ—

March 30, 2016

"I remember sitting in my room, afraid to go out"

I am at the Mission Hills Country Club in Rancho Mirage in California.

It is the first major championship of the Ladies Professional Golf Association, and I have been invited to play in the pro-amateur the day before the ANA Inspiration tournament begins. Danielle Kang, a good friend over the years, is the pro. Abby Wambach is one of the amateurs: she helped keep me from tripping at the ESPY awards nine months earlier in my first public appearance. I will always be indebted to her for that.

The sad sack snoops make note of what I am wearing: a purple skirt that is described as a micro mini when the fact is that all professional golfers wear a skirt above the knee to effectively hit the ball, a white quarter-zip sweatshirt (in other words, a standard golf jacket), and a white visor. They call me "sexy" as if I dressed up for the occasion when all I am doing is trying to play golf in an outfit that was given to me by Kang. I didn't even pick it out. Plus, what really pisses me off is that most of them don't mention my game, because I am on fire, folks.

I love golf. For many years it was my therapy, playing on the Sherwood Country Club course in Thousand Oaks, California, to have some peace and get away from the endless chaos of the Kardashian household filled with camera crews and fashion fitters and repairmen and everything else morning, noon, and night. I still love golf, more than ever since my transition. I always used to play alone, too awkward and uncomfortable to play with others. But now I join other golfers. Plus Sherwood, as high-end as it is conservative, changed its locker room policy without a bit of fuss or drama.

I wondered how Caitlyn would hit a golf ball as compared to Bruce, since Bruce hit it pretty darn good, 280 yards off the tee when the groove was right.

The pro-am answers the question.

Not only can Caitlyn still hit the crap out of the ball, but her short game has improved.

I score an eagle on the very first hole of the Dinah Shore Tournament Course, nailing it from 122 yards out. This time at least one media outlet is where it needs to be. The Golf Channel is covering the event, and for the next two days, it shows the shot over and over.

I am spending the night at the Westin hotel in Rancho Mirage, where there will be a party for the tournament later that night. It brings me back four or five years earlier, when I had stayed at the same Westin. It was the familiar routine back then of having to give a speech and finding a little window for the woman inside me to surface. So I got there the night before: after the now-familiar rite of surveying the hotel like a cat burglar, I made the delightful discovery that this was a great place in which I could dress as I desired and walk around as long as I made sure to get a room on the ground floor. Which of course I did.

The rooms had sliding glass doors, which meant you could just go out the back and walk around at night outside with minimal lighting.

I brought several outfits because I wasn't sure of what I was going to wear. I felt the pulse of fun and anticipation of getting dressed as usual.

I heard a party going on. I went to the sliding glass door to look. It was a lesbian-only affair, and there were several hundred. I heard them talk and I saw them laugh and I saw the ease with which they interacted. I saw them dress the way they wanted to dress, and wear their hair the way they wanted. They had freedom, such beautiful freedom. I could not take my eyes off them. If there was ever a group that was understanding toward me, this would be it. I wondered if there were some trans women among them.

I desperately wanted to slide those glass doors open and walk out into the mix of them. I just wanted to say "hi" in one of my outfits, have a glass of wine, and take in the new world like a revolving carousel. The hell with that: I would have led the party because I had been voted best dancer at Newtown High. Instead I snuck out in my outfit in the opposite direction. I did my brief lobby walk-through and then I went back to the room. The party still beckoned with its peals of laughter. God, they were having a good time. I should have been there, just do it, just walk into the room and let them figure out who I am.

But I was afraid. Afraid of what I was always afraid of. Getting caught. Being discovered. Subjecting my family to shame. Destroying what reputation I had left. I could not do it. Between *Keeping Up with the Kardashians* and some cosmetic surgery and growing my hair long, the sad sack snoops were already all over me at this point in the early 2010s. I could envision the immediate assumption they would make about the party because it was all female:

BRUCE JENNER CROSS-DRESSES AT A LESBIAN EVENT

The headline would have gone around the world.

Twice.

So I just sat in my room and continued to listen, the party like the sun on the horizon, eventually shutting down. Sitting on the bed with my hands clasped, trapped behind the sliding glass door, still closed because I was too terrified to open it, I couldn't help but feel that I would do the same, carve out a life and somehow try to live with myself until I just shut down.

Now I am back at the Westin after transition with nothing to hide. No more sneaking around whenever I could, looking forward and backward over both shoulders. No more walking the fairway in loneliness and isolation, a great lay-up to the green with no one else around to admire it, a golf cart always for one.

I will go to the party tonight. Many of the top players in the LPGA are going to be there. I will have that glass of wine I was too afraid to have and be the self I was too afraid to be. My life is so much simpler now: I do what I want to do when I want to do it.

Just for the record, Danielle Kang and I won the pro-am portion of the tournament.

A month and a half later, in the middle of May 2016, I go to Las Vegas for the SkyBridge Alternatives Conference, known as SALT, a remarkable conclave of political leaders and hedge fund titans and top policy makers.

As Bruce, I always liked going to Vegas, not for the gambling or the garishness but because it was the best place of all to dress up, the only locale where you could do whatever you wanted and no one would notice. So I became almost giddy when there was a speech scheduled in Vegas. As I told Kris back in those days:

I'm off to Vegas!

Have fun!

Oh, I will.

As always, I had my routine down to perfection.

I left the house in Hidden Hills. Almost immediately I drove to the back of a nearby parking lot. I applied makeup in the car, then tried on several wigs I kept hidden underneath the backseat and picked out the one that not only suited my mood but best concealed my identity. Next came putting on a favored outfit while still inside the car. Then five hours of blissful driving through hot and lonely desert, until I got to a Holiday Inn parking lot on the Vegas outskirts and wiped all the makeup off and removed the wig and wiggled out of the clothes.

I checked into my hotel room and did everything all over again. There can't possibly be a place in the world that has more mirrors per hotel room than Vegas. Which is why I brought more than one outfit, since it was so much fun to try them on.

Then right before the speech I once again took everything off. The next day for the ride home, I put on minimal makeup and very dark sunglasses. I got back into the car, scanned for bystanders, and applied the rest of my makeup and put on another wig to disguise my identity and dressed in another outfit. Then I drove back across the desert to the same parking lot five minutes from the house where I took everything off and once again hid it. Then I went home like nothing happened.

How'd it go?
Fine.
Anything new?
Same old same old.
It must get boring.
Never.

The only problem with the Vegas routine was the Starbucks issue. I needed my grande vanilla latte, and there was one on the way back near Barstow. It meant going in dressed up or taking everything off again. So I drove on by. But I still missed the fix. I thought about it a lot, how I couldn't even get a cup of coffee the way I wanted. Finally, during an appearance in Lake Las Vegas, I had enough.

I got dressed up early in the morning and walked to the nearest Starbucks. I ordered, the first time I can ever recall having an actual encounter with someone while in women's clothing. I disguised my voice as best I could.

I'll have a grande vanilla latte.

Anything else?

No, that's it.

For the first time in my life I hoped there would be no more conversation.

She told me the amount. I paid her and she gave me my change with the same cheerful expression she gave to everyone else. A few minutes later the barista handed me my grande vanilla latte.

God, that felt good. Even if it happened only once before I became Caitlyn.

Now, several years later, I am at the SALT conference. I am staying at the Bellagio and walking through the casino with a great outfit on. The atmosphere is the same as it was a few months earlier at the Westin. People stop me and talk to me and want to take selfies. They are genuinely excited to see me, and that gives me great gratification and strength. I can make a difference. I have made a difference. I love how they come up to me, their voices alive in excitement:

Caitlyn! Caitlyn!

God, that feels good.

All the time.

—⟋⟍—

Chapter Ten

Bye Bye Breasts

I will never get out of my mind Linda's reaction when she saw me dressed up in women's clothing in the New York hotel room for the first and only time. She was shocked, and shocked would have been okay. Sometimes you adjust to shock. It was much more how uncomfortable she was, how she could barely look at me, and when she did her eyes were somewhere else, desperate to avoid any direct contact. Linda wanted to be supportive. Linda wanted to understand. But it was all too much, and I in turn felt not simply freakish but dirty and indecent, a screwed-up weirdo unable to control his impulses, inflicting himself on others who wanted no part. We had had our differences. The marriage could not be saved, but in that room I felt she was revolted by me. I know she did not mean to, but her reaction was my greatest fear realized.

With Kris it is different. It is different because unlike with Linda, who I never told a single thing until we had been married for several years, I talked to Kris about my issues very early in our relationship. She knows there is something inside me that must have a place to go. I blindsided Linda when I dressed up. She had no time to prepare and get emotionally ready, and neither did I, for that matter. Kris and I talk. She is willing to see what it feels like. So the first time I dress up in front of her, she seems comfortable. But I am the one who is uncomfortable, the memory of Linda's reaction still fresh even though it was roughly six years ago.

I get the feeling that Kris is willing to let me crossdress on certain occasions only because this is what I want. She has no real interest, and it's kind of ridiculous of me to think that she would. So I stop after a few times. It is easier and causes fewer problems.

She married Bruce. It is Bruce whose career she is trying to resuscitate. She has defended Bruce to her friends who have heard the rumors.

Eventually Kris and I do reach an understanding—take Caitlyn on the road—but she is not to play in our home or hometown. End of discussion.

I am okay with that. I can handle it. The excitement of a new marriage and the resurgence of family and career are energizing. It really is a partnership of equals—I am the product and Kris the agent and manager and negotiator. She is indefatigable and also undaunted: if someone says no, she doesn't get discouraged or take it personally but simply believes that she was talking to the wrong person. And trust me on this, she will find the right person, no matter how long it takes. When somebody approaches me about a business deal, I listen and say, "You have to talk to my manager about it," and silently wish him or her good luck because they are going to need it if they think they are going to outnegotiate Kris. It makes me relieved that I am just the product.

Kris and I and all the kids are truly one big happy family in the early 1990s. It is a profound moment of my life, the most profound moment. I am a father, a real father, not a pretend one or a preoccupied one or a selfish one, no matter how well meaning. Kris has welcomed Burt and Casey and Brandon and Brody into our lives with loving and gracious arms. Their moms have custody, but they visit regularly. Kris adores my kids as much as I adore her kids, another aspect of our partnership.

But the complexities of divorce make things difficult. Linda married David Foster, a very successful record producer, also in 1991. I felt that both Linda and I had successfully managed to get on with our lives. Our divorce settlement had been reached quickly without acrimony.

Then in the mid 1990s Linda files for support payments with the Los Angeles Superior Court. It was her right and prerogative under California law (the case is ultimately settled with a minimal monthly payment, and I don't think much of anything was achieved except legal fees).

We are initially subpoenaed late at night. Kris is upset, very upset, that her efforts to be a good stepmother are not appreciated. She is no longer inclined to make the effort. She also feels that both Linda and Chrystie really don't want the kids to be with us. Every time she invites them to do something, she feels there is some excuse as to why they can't come. When asked many years later, the Jenner kids have a different viewpoint: Kris just did not want them around anymore once we had our own children, fierce in her belief that I had only one family now and that was her and the Kardashians. Linda and Chrystie say they never did anything to stop our kids from spending time with Kris and me.

An entire book can be written on who did what to whom without any agreement or resolution. Everybody has a version, including me.

None of which matters, anyway.

Burt and Casey and Brandon and Brody are my children, and it was incumbent upon me to see them and make them part of my life regardless of what others wanted or didn't want. The kids are a part of my life, and I had to do whatever it took to make them a part of my life. I needed to assert myself. But I could not. So I let go of them, which is a softer way of saying I abandoned them. Because I did abandon them.

I begin to see less and less of the Jenner children. As the years go by I barely see them at all. My parental efforts are concentrated entirely on the raising of the Kardashian children and then Kendall and Kylie. I miss birthdays with the Jenner kids. I miss graduations, either because I am not invited or am invited and just don't come. Burt idolizes the rugged and daring image of Bruce, and I piss on it. When Casey gets married in 2007, I am not invited. Nor should I have been, given my prolonged absence from her life starting at the very beginning when I wasn't there for her birth.

I cope the way I so often cope with things. I block the kids from my mind, almost as if they exist only as an abstraction, part of someone else's life. I also don't want to argue with Kris. I don't want to argue with Linda and Chrystie. I cannot deal with any kind of confrontation. I run from it. Confrontation leaves me terribly wounded and even more insecure and filled with self-doubt than I already am. I am scared of asserting myself and often try to deflect with a humorous quip.

The Jenner kids have loving mothers and stepfathers. So maybe that's what I tell myself: they are doing fine and don't really need me. It is another way of coping with my guilt in not fighting as hard as I should have to see them when they were growing into their adolescence and young adulthood. I employ my now-ingrained psychological mechanism when I am faced with something emotionally wrenching: I act as if I am powerless, that it wasn't my fault, there was nothing I could do. I make myself a helpless victim.

I do the same with my sister, who has been such a mainstay in my life and whom I have adored since I was little. When Kris threw a party to celebrate the twentieth anniversary of my Olympic win, Pam was not invited. Neither was my mother (my dad was). Pam was devastated. Out of deference to me she had not told a single soul of my gender dysphoria for roughly a decade, although it only made it that much harder for her to process it. Kris had not wanted her there—a reaffirmation that the only family that should matter to me now was her family—and I went along with the decision. It created a terrible rupture between Pam and me. We rarely spoke for almost twenty years.

I could blame my gender dysphoria for what happened. There is a tendency to blame everything that goes south in your life on gender dysphoria. Insecurity and self-doubt do envelop you. But none of that somehow justifies abandoning your own children, some of them for roughly a decade, or the sister you idolized growing up. Then it's just a sad excuse and yet, it's the excuse I told myself.

If God refuses to make peace with me, this will be the primary reason.

It should be.

In 1995 Kendall comes into our lives. It is an incredible moment, one that at a certain point we thought would never happen. I have been off hormone therapy for several years. But one of the possible side effects of therapy is that you shoot blanks, so to speak. Actually, you aren't shooting much of anything. Kris and I discussed it and then together consulted with an endocrinologist, who after examination said that everything had returned to normal now that I had stopped the therapy.

Kendall will go on to become a young woman of poise and beauty and kindness, the most down-to-earth of all the K girls and a little bit of a daredevil athlete like her father. She handles the fame she has already had in her life with steadiness, as at home at a riding stable as she is walking the catwalk for Chanel. Kylie follows twenty-one months later, as incredible as her sister but with a distinctly different personality: fiery and exotic beauty, headstrong and like her mother, with a sixth sense for business.

After Kris gets pregnant with Kendall I become increasingly concerned about the breasts. I worry that I won't even be able to go to a swimming pool because they are so obviously noticeable.

These are not man boobs, folks. These are breasts. You don't go to a plastic surgeon to get man boobs removed. Imagine your own father having them while continuing to maintain that he is a man.

Actually, don't.

I talk to Kris about it. We go to a Beverly Hills plastic surgeon. He takes pictures of my chest and my paranoia is such that I worry that somehow some way they are going to get out, even though they are taken from the shoulders down so nobody would know who the hell it was anyway. But this is my thinking, always scared and terrified of discovery.

I tell him they are the residue of steroid use, a condition known as gynecomastia. Which of course is a lie: I have never taken any steroids in my life. But at this point I am willing to sully my own reputation.

The procedure is easy. He basically liposuctions them out, and from the vantage point of looking like a "normal" father I do look much better. But from the vantage point of myself I am sad for months afterward. I liked having them. Not only did they make me feel good about myself; I feel that my chest always should have been that way.

On the other hand, trying to hide them has become a pain in the neck. On windy days I am constantly pulling my shirt down so you can't see them. On one occasion I am walking across the street with Kris and the shirt is loose and I keep grabbing at it.

I know what you're doing.

Yeah, I don't want anybody to see them.

So as sad as I am to get rid of them, it is the only thing to do. I am stuck in Bruce mode forever, and that's that. Turn your focus elsewhere. I love being a father and stepfather to the Kardashians and Kendall and Kylie. I love raising kids. I love watching them grow up, taking them on trips, carpooling, anything and everything. It is my life in the 1990s and 2000s and 2010s, although I always know that no matter how much I try to block it out, there are four other wonderful children I have left behind.

It is because of Kris that my social life expands, leading to a bizarre and ultimately horrifying relationship for both of us. She is extremely close with Nicole Brown Simpson, which also means that O.J. comes into my life. I already know him a little bit, and a little bit goes a very long way because of his endless braggadocio. We have both come out of the same world of the male athlete with all its stereotypes and behavioral expectations, a type of identity that I come to call the male athlete gender.

I struggled against it because of my issues and extreme discomfort in that world and its constant objectification of women, and the endless bragging about fucking to the point where you had to wonder what these guys were really hiding. O.J. was at the completely opposite side of the spectrum as me—women as eye candy and sex toys, physically abusive when he did not get his way or felt he was being defied, the loud life of the party anywhere and anytime, like so many other athletes.

I did not care when my fame faded in the 1980s. I was consumed by something far more important. Fame was never important to me, except as a means to an end in having a career. O.J. could not bear the thought of losing his fame. So he behaved the way the male athlete too often behaves, doing anything he could to draw attention to himself. I saw countless male athletes like O.J. They were not as extreme, but their need for power and fame and public spectacle became even more intense after their careers because they knew it was the only way to not be what they feared the most: forgotten.

For all our profound personal differences, our careers had shared many similarities.

He seized the attention of the nation when he played football at the University of Southern California, capped off with a Heisman Trophy and the indelible image of him running for a sixty-four-yard touchdown to beat UCLA in 1967 in one of the greatest college football games of all time. It put him high atop a public pedestal that only grew higher when he played pro football for the Buffalo Bills and set a single-season rushing record in 1973 with 2003 yards. I likewise seized the attention of the nation when I won the decathlon, capped off with setting a world record on live television and the indelible image of the victory lap I took waving the American flag. We both became the faces of major brands, O.J. with Hertz and I with Wheaties. We both became sportscasters for ABC and later NBC. We both did motivational speeches. We both had modest film careers. We were both on the charity golf and tennis tournament circuit. We both knew what it was like to feel that pedestal, like a block of ice, begin to melt and the inevitability that others will take our places.

Because we had much in common, there perhaps should have been a lot for us to share and talk about. But there wasn't. We may have been of the same world, but we were not in the same world. If I looked in the mirror and loathed myself, I looked at O.J. and saw a monster of a male athlete. I wonder if this contributed to my feelings of awkwardness around him, that even if he embodied an archetype I hated, it was also the archetype that people expected from me.

There were other contributing factors in my distaste for him: he was the most narcissistic, egocentric, neediest asshole in the world of sports I had ever seen, and I had seen a lot of them.

I first met O.J. at the US Olympic Trials in Eugene, Oregon, in 1976. I was competing and he was broadcasting. I saw him after that at a charity tennis tournament in Forest Hills when we were both invited as celebrities. I always found him affable, but I also felt he was trying with every fiber of his soul to be affable. The more I saw of him, the more I felt he was never genuine. I eventually found him exhausting and pathetic, his need for one-upmanship such that it was almost like he was on the football field again in which everyone else was an opponent. I was always wary.

Kris's relationship to O.J. also went back a long time. He had been an usher at her wedding to Robert Kardashian in 1978. When Kris first mentioned O.J. to me, the marriage between him and Nicole was fundamentally over. Kris told me that Nicole hated him to such a degree that she once had said to her:

Every time he gets on a plane I hope it crashes.

The week after Kris shared Nicole's comment with me, I saw O.J. at the Robert F. Kennedy charity golf tournament in Hyannis Port, Massachusetts. He was practicing putts. He was friendly, but he also had to know that Kris and I were dating and that Kris had probably told me about the dark depth of his relationship with Nicole. Right away as we exchanged pleasantries I could see him going into the male athlete mode of "everything is perfect because I'm supposed to be perfect." He was also putting on a show for me, wanting me to think that everything between him and Nicole was cool. I was cordial, as I always am.

So, how's everything going with you?

Hey, when your wife's happy, you're happy.

Wait a second. I thought:

Your wife just told Kris she wishes you were dead. So it can't be that good.

I continued the conversation just to get it over with.

Hey, that's great.

It became even stranger when O.J. said he had taken a Lear jet from New York for the tournament and it was so crowded that he had to sit on the toilet in the back. He made fun of it, and I laughed along with him, but once again I was thinking something very different.

That would have made your wife even happier.

The pathological need of O.J. to still be the big man on campus came sharply into focus when we were in New Orleans to cover the 1992 US Olympic trials for NBC. All the broadcasters used earpieces so the lead producer could communicate with us during the event. During commercial breaks, a song that was popular at the time by Salt-N-Pepa came blaring through:

Let's talk about sex, baby!
Let's talk about you and me!

The song was like water torture after a while. It stuck to your brain. It was driving me berserk. It was driving everyone berserk. Except O.J., belting out the lyrics every time it came on. Others laughed but I found it sad, this desperation to be noticed, the need for cheers in any situation.

Kris was in town with me, so we made plans with O.J. to have dinner that night at a vintage New Orleans French restaurant. We got there early. All I wanted to do was be discreet, get in and get dinner and get out without attention since I was still frequently recognized. The restaurant—I think it was Galatoire's—had a steady hum, and that was the sound of eating remarkable food. A thousand great and famous dignitaries and celebrities had eaten there.

O.J. walked in fifteen minutes later with his posse.

His notion of quiet was to sing at the top of his lungs:

Let's talk about sex, baby!
Let's talk about you and me!

If you didn't know Juice was in the house, you surely would now. The singing also had the desired effect: other diners turned in their chairs and started yelling "Juice! Juice!" (so much for the uninterrupted sound of eating). He kept on singing like a downtown Vegas casino act.

We finished dinner and walked out onto Bourbon

Street. The street was noisy. It was hard to imagine any-one wanting to make it noisier—except O.J., who was loud and boisterous and needed the crowd yelling "Juice! Juice! Juice!" just like he was back playing UCLA.

We stopped in front of a strip club. The line was thirty deep. As many people recognized me as they did O.J., but I was not about to crash the line. They had been waiting. Not O.J. He went right by high-fiving people as he walked right in. Once again the cries of "Juice! Juice!"

I had never been to a place like this. I know I was supposed to like it, because that is an essential part of the male athlete, stripper poles and revolving balls of light. I hated such clubs because whatever money the workers made, I could only assume, based on stories from other athletes, was from an interaction that was always demean-ing women and ogling them and trying to grope them. The idea of getting a lap dance even for the hell of it was sickening to me. But it was also a slippery slope, because I could not seem to be turned off.

I tried to act as comfortable as possible, at least as if I was amused. But once again it only heightened for me the assumptions of gender that society imposes upon us, women this way and men that way and the male athlete a species unto himself. All I had to do was look at O.J. to see those expectations fulfilled, drinking and laughing and having lap dances like nobody's business.

Much of my interaction with O.J. was on the golf course. I am a good golfer, and O.J. wasn't. It drove him crazy that I was better, his macho core such that he always had to win at everything. Which is probably why he lied about the number of strokes he had taken and kicked the ball to get a better lie when he thought nobody was looking. I made small talk one time by mentioning a company I had signed with, and O.J. immediately said, *Oh yeah, I know the CEO, we are really good friends.* After a while I never brought up anything because I knew O.J.'s inevitable response would be that he had done it first and he had done it better. I could not imagine being married to him and having to feed his insatiable ego day in and day out. The more I learned, the more obvious it became that the slightest thing set him off.

About six months before the 1994 murders, Kris and I hosted our annual Christmas Eve party. Nicole and O.J. at this point had been divorced for a little over a year. But Kris and I wanted to be friendly, so we invited both of them on the assumption they would bring their two children. We had also invited a friend named Joseph Perulli, who had dated Nicole after the divorce.

O.J. hated Perulli. When Perulli left Nicole's house, he would sometimes see O.J. down the street watching in his car. So Kris called Perulli.

Listen, O.J. is coming. Maybe you should not come.

I have a gift to drop off. I will just get there early.

O.J. came to the party with Nicole and their children before the other guests. He was in good spirits, hugs all around. We always had Santa Claus come, and the kids were excited. Since it was early we were relieved that Perulli had decided not to come at all. Then he walked in. O.J. was in the entryway by the front door when he saw him.

Hi.

He went into the living room. Kris came up to me. She was very nervous, which she almost never gets, as was Nicole.

Go in the other room. Talk to O.J. We are getting Joseph out of here.

I went into the living room, where there were two couches opposite one another with a coffee table in the middle. I sat down. O.J. was just staring ahead. I looked at him to see if anything would register and it did not. I tried to engage him.

Hey O.J., have you played any golf recently?

Nothing. Not a blink of the eye. Nothing. I had never been with anybody with such a reaction, or more precisely a nonreaction, like that. He literally was not there. I could not get up and leave without trying one more time.

Hey, O.J. I'm off Thursday. Want to play golf?

Nothing.

I left and found Kris.

This is the strangest thing I have ever seen in my life. He's like not even there. I asked him some questions, and he was staring into space.

O.J. got up, found Nicole and the kids, and essentially grabbed them.

We're leaving.

Several months after the party, Kris and I were in bed watching the news at around ten thirty p.m. when we got a call from Nicole.

Where's Kris?

She's right here.

Put her on the line.

She wanted to talk to both of us, so we placed the call on speaker. We had a mutual friend named Faye Resnick. She was great when she was sober but also had a cocaine problem and a very addictive personality. We had not seen her for a while, so we were concerned something was up. Nicole confirmed it.

Faye got back into drugs, and if she doesn't stop she's going to kill herself. She will just keep taking drugs until she dies. We need to have an intervention. We have to get a group together who knows her and do it tonight.

Tonight?

She has to be in rehab by the morning. That's our goal.

We got dressed and went to Starbucks to get some coffee and picked up Nicole at her house. Then we went to Faye's.

We walked in and there was Faye, and I wished all my children could have been here to see what drugs can do. Faye was a thin, attractive woman who always cared about the way she looked. But now she was completely disheveled and had lost thirty pounds and was almost skeletal.

There were about six or seven of us who gathered,

including her ex-husband and ex-boyfriend. We all were fundamentally saying the same thing:

Faye, you have to go to rehab.

Oh, I'm fine.

We went through her purse and found cocaine. We started cleaning up the house, which was a mess.

Over and over, Nicole kept saying the same thing to Faye:

If you don't stop, you're going to die. And you don't want your daughter to grow up without a mother.

I was listening to the urgency and sincerity and love in Nicole's voice. She, more than anyone else in my mind, was the one who got her to rehab.

Three or maybe four days afterward, Nicole was dead.

Still to this day, I wish we had known that the person we needed to save in that room at that very moment was Nicole. As serious as Faye's situation was, Nicole's was even more life-threatening:

It was her children who would grow up without a mother.

I was in Chicago playing in a celebrity golf tournament on June 13, 1994, when somebody drove up to me in a cart and said I had to call home because there was an emergency. I instantly feared someone in the family had gotten hurt. I immediately called Kris, who was crying over the phone.

Nicole is dead…Nicole is dead…Nicole is dead…

What?

You have to come home right away.

Kris did not know the circumstances, whether it was a robbery or home invasion or what. I threw my stuff into my suitcase and headed for the airport. I did not know until later that O.J. had been in Chicago as well playing in a different golf tournament. I did not know that until after the murders of Nicole and Ron Goldman the night of June 12, 1994, he had left for the Windy City the same night, presumably to give himself an alibi.

When I got to the ticket counter, the agent recognized me and smiled and casually uttered what would turn out to be the creepiest thing ever said to me, a chilling reminder that no matter how different O.J. and I were, people would always perceive us as being from the same male athlete gender mold, recognizable celebrities because of our sports accomplishments, peas in the same pod.

Oh, O.J. had to get back to Los Angeles, too.

I have tried to erase O.J. from my mind. Everybody I know has. I believe he got away with two savage murders, but the trial caused enormous tension within the family because of all the improbably woven strands. Kris and I, knowing the background of O.J. and Nicole and her hatred and fear of him, believed he had done it the minute we heard of her murder and the circumstances surrounding it. Because of Robert Kardashian's relationship to O.J.— being on his defense team and one of his longstanding friends—Robert's daughters Kourtney and Kim were on O.J.'s side (Khloé was too young to really understand).

The case was impossible to discuss, two daughters firm in the conviction that he hadn't done it because of their father's involvement, and their mother and stepfather firm in the conviction that he had done it. When O.J. was found not guilty, Kourtney came into the house after school and said to me:

See, I told you he didn't do it.

I am always cognizant of my role of stepfather, but this was one of the rare moments where I just stepped in without checking with Robert first, because that simply wasn't possible given his role in the trial. I took both Kourtney and Kim aside privately and explained to them that a jury finding of not guilty did not mean that O.J. was innocent of two murders. I also said to them:

The name of O.J. Simpson will never be mentioned in this house again.

It wasn't.

But it still lingered in so many different ways, because he would always haunt us.

I always wondered why Robert Kardashian was so aligned with O.J. They had both gone to the University of Southern California, Robert had helped him on business deals, and there was no doubt that their friendship was deep and sincere and that they both saw admirable qualities in one another. But his defense of O.J. was so extreme given Robert's impeccable character. When I tried to sort it out, I wondered if it somehow had to do with Kris.

The divorce still devastated Robert. Everybody knew that. And now Kris at that point in the 1990s was appearing in hundreds of infomercials with me, looking lean and fit and happy as we promoted our exercise equipment. I wondered if Robert saw all this and began to think she was becoming something of a celebrity and it ate away at him—until the O.J. case, when he became a superstar and completely overshadowed her. All of a sudden he was the one all over TV, and I wonder if it was his way of saying to her what I think she was saying to him when she married me: a big *fuck you*.

Long after the trial and the verdict of not guilty, Robert and I were in the car one day. We had always been friendly to one another and liked one another. We talked all the time about parenting. We never talked much about the trial. The look of shock on his face when O.J. was acquitted had become famous because of its very indication that he was shocked by the verdict. In a subsequent interview with Barbara Walters on ABC's *20/20*, he did admit that he had doubts about the verdict in light of the blood evidence against Simpson. But that was as far as he went.

I don't even know why the trial came up in our conversation. At that point there had been two of them, the criminal trial in Los Angeles Superior Court and the civil trial in the same court in which a jury quickly concluded that O.J. had done it and held him liable for millions of dollars in worthless damages because he didn't have any money. The hysteria had died down, so maybe Robert felt comfortable. Or maybe his guard was down. Or maybe he didn't care anymore. But he turned and said to me:

I would've been okay with it if they had gotten him in the first trial.

The implication was obvious that he believed O.J. was guilty. But there is no way of knowing now what he exactly meant, since he tragically died of cancer in 2003 at the age of fifty-nine. Just as there was no way of him knowing that the name Kardashian would one day become a pop culture phenomenon all over the world. Or that his children and Kris would collectively become impossibly famous.

Or that his ex-wife's husband would one day be called Caitlyn.

—◊—

April 4, 2016

"It was only a game"

I am in Eugene.

I am returning to one of the most legendary track and field facilities in the world on the University of Oregon campus. The Nike shoe was invented here by the then Oregon track coach Bill Bowerman and Phil Knight, a middle distance runner at the university. I cannot possibly match such accomplishments. But I was invented here as well, the first time the name of Bruce Jenner became associated with the Olympics. I came out of nowhere in 1972 when I finished third in the US Olympic Trials. I never went back to nowhere again as an athlete.

I am here for *Sports Illustrated*. They are doing a cover story on the fortieth anniversary of my win in the 1976 games. Some of the photographs are being taken by Heinz Kluetmeier, who also shot pictures of me competing in the Games for the magazine.

AWRRIGHT! read the headline of the magazine cover in

capital yellow letters after I won, looking as tall as Times Square neon. Beneath: BRUCE JENNER WINS BIG.

The story will be part of *Sports Illustrated*'s "Where Are They Now?" issue appearing in July 2016, featuring such other athletes as Ken Griffey Jr., Drew Bledsoe, and William Perry. There are about a dozen of us named in all. We have all traveled a long way from then to now, some more remembered than others. But it is safe to say that none of the other male athletes honored now wear a blouse or a dress or a gown or a pantsuit (at least in public).

I am sitting at the end of a long bench at Hayward Field, painted in the dark green of the University of Oregon colors. It isn't a field but a track and field shrine, with seating for 10,500, and the host of the US Olympic Trials six times, including 1972 and 1976, when I competed. The Nike origins only add to the legend: from a track shoe inspired by a waffle iron into a company with a market capitalization of $100.1 billion.

It is early morning and the sun is rising. I am in the cold of shadow and then the warmth of light, and while I prefer the light better I am not uncomfortable with the shadow since I spent so much of my life there. I am gazing out onto the oval of the track, sitting on a bench. It is the pose of pondering that photographers and magazine editors resort to to suggest reflection and the ooze of nostalgia over past triumphs since I had three distinct ones here.

I cooperate with the producer, who is doing a

companion video for Sports Illustrated Films to the written piece by Tim Layden. There are several videographers and, of course, Heinz.

I was on a mission to make something out of myself after finishing third here in the trials in 1972 and being such an unknown that the *New York Times* misidentified me in its wrap-up. In 1975 I set a world record here. In the 1976 trials here before Montreal, I broke it. But it was all just a game. Just sports. Maybe that sounds dismissive: without my athletic accomplishments I would not be writing these words or no one would care if I were writing them. I know that.

It was only a game because of what I know now, what I feel now, that the only worthy self is the true self. It is not the sole province of those living their lives in the wrong gender, or those discovering their sexual preference, but in anyone who is different and feels different and wants to celebrate that difference as a natural outgrowth of our humanity, defined not by what others believe but the beautiful singularity of our hearts and souls.

If I ponder anything, it is not the past but my present and my future. Life is wonderful today as I have just passed my first anniversary after transition, although not without its conflicts and sometimes being a piñata for the media.

I am used to it, of course. They bother me for a little bit, and then the bother goes away. They are forgotten in the bottomless pit of the Internet. But sometimes they linger, and they do hurt and cause damage, and not just to me.

Like the story floated by a Canadian writer named Ian Halperin, in my mind desperately and pathetically trying to generate publicity for some silly book he wrote on the Kardashians. Halperin claimed in an interview that I was unhappy and considering transitioning back to Bruce. The story was one hundred percent wrong and garbage and swill. But the story went viral and was printed all over the world, including the *New York Times* and the *Washington Post*, without verification. They legitimized the story, making it seem like fact.

The other problem with these stories, the problem virtually everyone in the public spotlight faces, is that there is no recourse. So I want to make the point here one more time as emphatically as I can. I have never been happier. Transitioning back? It's the opposite.

Halperin's story has another pernicious effect. In church I met a teenager who wanted to transition but was having difficulty convincing his parents. I gave him my phone number so he could talk to an understanding voice. He called me one day and said that his father read the story about my alleged desire to transition back and was using it as ammunition against his son; in other words, the son would regret it just as Caitlyn Jenner regretted it. I can only convey to the father that the story is totally false. But who knows whether I will be believed or not. It would be a terrible tragedy if I'm not.

*　　*　　*

We move down to the track itself. The producer wonders if it is not impossible to want to run again or at least bounce around on the track a little bit. I do so in an exaggerated way so I purposely look clownish.

He wants me to say I miss being back here, what a big part of my life it was. I say the appropriate words, but my heart isn't in it. Actually, being on the track makes me realize how much I don't want to run at all. (It's the same with the shot I find when cleaning out the garage in Malibu. I look at it, think about picking it up for old time's sake, realize I have no interest in the shot put anymore, and roll it several feet into a corner.) I know it would be great for the cameras for a tear to come to my eye. But there is really no sense of nostalgia for me.

Bruce may be stuck here. And that's fine.

Caitlyn never was and never will be.

—⁂—

Chapter Eleven

No Way Out

Kris and I are watching a television show on MTV one night called *The Osbournes*. It is about a family of four living in Beverly Hills, presided over by Ozzy Osbourne, a heavy metal god whose days of biting off the heads of bats at raucous concerts are behind him. The show is amusing: watching Ozzy in a domesticated role as a father and husband has its moments. He seems like he is intoxicated half the time, and he later admits he *was* intoxicated all the time during the shooting of each episode from 2002 to 2005.

Under our own roof we now have six children, five daughters and a son. The house is awash in puberty and adolescence and young adulthood and two parents with very different styles. It seems to me something is there for television.

Kris says she is the one who came up with the idea and decided to actively pitch it to Ryan Seacrest, the host of the enormously popular *American Idol* and a television producer looking for projects...

Kris knows Seacrest. A meeting is held with him and he loves the concept. The next step is to meet with the E! network's vice president of original programming, Lisa Berger. She is not so in love.

I don't know if I get it. The only person in the room I know of is Bruce.

Seacrest keeps pushing. In 2007 Berger gives a tepid green light for four episodes, largely because I am in the public eye and maybe that's a hook. It is now in its twelfth season and the most successful reality show in the history of television.

Everybody in my family has a different personality that is incorporated into the show. I am the well-meaning but confused and helpless father and husband. I get love but very little respect. I'm fine with that, because it is largely accurate. Plus I have stood on the public platform earlier in my life. I don't need that anymore. The women on the show want to be out front, and that is cool with me.

I rarely watch unless I am actively involved in an episode. I know that my mother is embarrassed, as are other members of her family. In 2008 my aunt Ellie sends a letter to Kris and me to our home in Hidden Hills:

What a disappointment you are to your public, Bruce. I haven't heard one complimentary thing from anyone yet. The consensus is that you look like a "milky-toast" and "henpecked husband" and stepfather. You do look very uncomfortable in every scene you are in.

The implication is that I have sold myself out, willingly destroyed what positive reputation I have left.

Pretty much on the mark.

I still feel weak and inferior. I still have no self-respect. I feel as trapped in the middle between male and female as I ever have been. So maybe it's only fitting that I am treated on the show like a new version of electrolysis without painkillers: reality-show humiliation. But I don't care. The impetus for doing it is that the money generated will create a healthy trust fund for all the Kardashian kids and especially for Kendall and Kylie. I hope the exposure parlays into something bigger, which it does: there is no family that is better known not just in America but maybe the world, given that the show is aired in 150 countries and all the kids have branched out so far beyond it.

If it seems like Kris intimidates me at times, that's because she does. She was confident and sure of herself when I met her and becomes even more so as the show takes off. With me, it's the flip side: I am more lacking in confidence and unsure of myself than I was when I met her. But I also wonder if the public's perceptions of both of us are based on stereotypic roles of male and female behavior. The male in the household is supposed to be assertive, in control, the captain, particularly if the male is an Olympic gold medalist. Because I am not, I am labeled weak. Kris, on the other hand, as the female in the household, is supposed to be subservient, nonaggressive, letting the male make all the major decisions. Because she is not, she is often labeled as an overbearing bitch. We both play against expected gender type, and to a certain degree we are targeted for it.

From a deeply personal standpoint, *Keeping Up with the Kardashians* is a demarcation for Kris and me. I believe that the more successful it becomes, the less she needs me. I am not the primary breadwinner anymore. I feel increasingly irrelevant. I receive a healthy paycheck for doing the show, and I continue to do speeches, but I never see a dime of it: it all goes right to Kris. Plus, what I make is nothing compared to the kids because of all their other ventures. Kris, in addition to being the show's executive producer, also takes a 10 percent cut from the Kardashian kids as the so-called Momager (she trademarked the title in 2015).

I do not have a checking account. I have a credit card, but purchases are carefully pored over. Kris is incredibly generous—on her own terms. She buys me a Porsche after I express interest in getting one but know I can't (she does put the title in her name). She buys me a membership to the exclusive Sherwood for somewhere around $200,000 so I can play golf. They are amazing gestures, but it is becoming increasingly difficult for me not to make any financial decisions on my own.

Actually, I can't make any.

What keeps me going, what always kept me going during much of the twenty-three years of marriage, was being a father to the Kardashians and Kendall and Kylie. I got heavily into carpooling, made tricky because at one point they attended several different schools. I often woke up at five thirty in the morning, then made sure the kids were fed and out the door by six thirty. Kourtney and Kim were going at the time to Marymount High School next to UCLA (Khloé had gone to a variety of schools, and I didn't always carpool her). I dropped them off in the thick of traffic, then returned home. I picked up Kendall and Kylie and took them to preschool in Bel Air, which meant going through the traffic I just came back from, LA traffic. I dropped them off and then had to pick them up at twelve thirty and bring them home. Then I had to drive all the way back to pick up Kourtney and Kim from Marymount and take them home. This particular routine went on for three years. Some days it took six hours. Welcome to the life I had made for myself.

But I liked it. It was an opportunity to talk to the kids. It also got me out of the house. Kris rarely carpooled, particularly as the business of managing the Kardashians became increasingly thriving and complex. She also had me to do the driving. The more successful Kardashian Inc. (which includes Kendall and Kylie), the more obvious it is that Kris wants me out of the house as much as possible, probably because I really do nothing when I am around and it drives her crazy.

The gender issues are percolating again by the late 2000s. More than ever I crave going on the road and doing my hotel routine. The rise of the Internet over the previous decade has also opened up a new world for me. I can read the personal stories of people wondering if they should transition and watch them on YouTube and realize I am not the only one going through such torment as they cope with their own gender dysphoria. I read about trans men and women who, now that they have transitioned, celebrate themselves and for the first time in their lives love themselves for who they are.

I watch the medical procedures that can be performed, including the Final Surgery. I wonder more than ever what it would like to get rid of my penis one day, this silly and useless lump of skin that irritates the hell out of me. But watching the surgery is not pleasant. I don't make it all the way through.

Another great benefit of the Internet is online shopping. I still need to be careful, so I don't go crazy. Since Kris screens my purchases, I use someone else's debit card. But I am lucky: if my family has more makeup per household than any in America, it also has more packages. How will they possibly notice a little one for me? But I am still paranoid. If there is one, I try to intercept it almost as soon as it is delivered. But sometimes I can't get there in time. Then Kris retrieves it.

Oh, this is for you.
Thanks.

A bullet dodged.

I buy a few items of clothing, a couple of bras. Mostly it is silicone forms for your breasts and hips and buttocks. Maybe this sounds easy to you, but it's not. My store of choice is the Breast Form Store. The selection is amazing on all fronts, but in breast forms alone there are such styles as Amoena, Amolux, Aphrodite, Divine, Gold Seal, NearlyMe, Platinum Seal, Silver Seal, and several more, not including ones for sleeping and travel and swimming. So it's complicated. You don't want one too small. You don't want one too big. Each of the breast styles has a different feel. Plus there are nipple styles to choose from.

Thank God I went to college.

When it comes to forms for the buttocks, I keep two sizes in my little closet—a small one and one a little bigger, depending on my mood. I also learn early on that the gel ones are much better than the padded ones. The gel ones look real. The padded ones look like you have padding.

After many years of experimentation and practice, I am really getting my routine down. To wear a wig right you need to tamp down and hide your hair as much as possible so that it almost feels like you are putting the wig on your bare skull. I have seen movies where people wear skullcaps before putting on wigs. But I don't know where to buy one, so I start using a stocking one of the kids or Kris has left lying around. Then I just start going to the grocery store—meats, vegetables, fish, cashews, and a couple of pairs of stockings and pantyhose "for the missus." Then I see on television the caps competitive swimmers wear, so I go to an athletic apparel store and buy a couple. They really work well and I think I have found the perfect solution, but to be honest they are a little tight around the cranium and become uncomfortable after a while.

Whatever I use—stocking or swimming cap—I tuck all my hair inside it and pull it over the ear and down in back so nothing is showing. Then I use a roll of clear packing tape I bought at the pharmacy and cut two pieces into three-inch strips. Then I tear them perfectly down the middle so now there are four strips, each a half inch in width. I carefully lay them on the counter so they don't get all tangled up and start sticking to one another. Then I apply a single drop of Krazy Glue to the end of each strip.

But never more than one drop!

The excess will seep everywhere if you apply more than one, and it will be a royal pain to clean up. I place the Krazy Glue end of the tape on my skin about a quarter-inch below the makeshift skullcap. I use a cloth to wipe off any excess, then apply the other end of the tape to the skullcap, smoothing it down as much as possible. This has the effect of getting rid of a lot of skin around the eyebrows by pushing the skin up. As I get older and jowls appear I also use the clear tape and Krazy Glue method behind the ear (don't pull too much, just a little). Then I use the tape and glue to give my forehead just a little lift. Finally I take a piece of tape and wrap it around the skullcap so nothing moves.

Voila!

A mini facelift, and it probably cost ten bucks.

I am proud to say my face looks pretty damn good and makes it very difficult for anyone to recognize me as Bruce. It has been achieved only after extensive trial and error. Many different styles of tapes are used. The Krazy Glue is quite genius, if I say so myself. I realized that when I sweat, none of the tape, no matter how sticky, would work. I could not afford to have my eyebrows suddenly start drooping down. So I searched for an alternative method, which is when it popped into my head that doctors sometimes use a similar substance on cuts instead of stitches.

There is only one drawback to Krazy Glue: it can sometimes stick to your skin so much that it takes a little piece of skin with it when you pull it off (another reason to be careful about how much you use!). This on occasion has created mysterious red dots on my forehead, but fortunately I have makeup to cover it.

After I perform my little facelift, I do my makeup. Then I put my wig on, which always has bangs so none of the clear strips show.

Another issue is waistline. You want a tight one. But men in general don't have a good one: our waist is too wide. Women have a much smaller waist area and more defined buttocks.

I buy a big box of clear plastic wrap (any brand will do). I take the roller out of the box. I start at my side and wrap it around my waist and lower chest four or five times. It has the effect of a girdle but is much thinner and lighter. Then I put on Spanx or something similar to further tighten.

Voilà!

I have taken four inches off my waist.

I look better and better, more and more like a woman, or more precisely the image I have of what I should look like as a woman.

But these are Band-Aids. I am becoming increasingly unhappy, feeling more and more worthless and invisible, sleepwalking through life until it is over. I also think about my dad, who died in 2000 at the age of seventy-seven. He had cancer and then it spread. I had a home in Lake Tahoe, California, at the time and he had been living there, his marriage to my mom ending in divorce after forty-one years. I wasn't in Tahoe when he died because I was on a business trip. Several days earlier I had come into his room.

I just want you to know that you are a really good dad. You raised great children, you were a really great inspiration to me.

I love you, son.

And I love you too, Dad.

He drifted off after this. I left the room and never saw him again. He was laid to rest at Arlington National Cemetery, where he had always hoped to be buried and where he belonged.

The last day I saw him, he said something else in a quiet whisper.

I never should've made it this long.

I knew he was talking about Omaha Beach and the sheer luck of surviving while so many others died. It stirred something inside me, not about war and duty and sacrifice but that there really isn't a second to waste in life, that you must do what you must do before it's too late and your luck is over.

Kris and I have been married for more than twenty years. The first fifteen or so were good and sometimes great. But the last five have been terrible, and I know that Kris in her heart of hearts will agree. The challenge for any marriage is that we constantly change as we grow older. For a successful marriage you have to grow together. We didn't come close.

We are at each other's throats. She is frustrated with me all the time. I am worn down. She yells and then I yell back because I always feel on the defensive. She resents that I never want to leave the house unless it means a hotel room somewhere, that I am content to sit around and watch the History Channel. She resents that I really don't do anything besides tapings for the show.

I don't feel like I am living anymore. I need control of my life back. I need control of my finances so I can spend money the way I want to. The house is like a train station, people in and out, out and in. I have no privacy to do what

I want to do when I want to do it. I am tired of taking it out on the road so I can spend an hour and a half to get dressed for fifteen minutes of freedom. I want to see my first four children without friction and the fear that it might upset Kris. I am tired of my life consisting of secret items tucked away in a tiny closet with a lock and key.

I cannot go on like this.

—m—

Chapter Twelve

Faith

I move into a house in Malibu on the ocean, a significant upgrade from my last rental there. I am alone. In the past I experienced such isolation and loneliness when I was alone, but I don't feel either of those now.

I feel free.

I have also started to try to repair my relationships with the four oldest Jenner children now that they are adults.

There is a lot to fix. I know that. But at least we are beginning to talk regularly. It is a blessed occurrence. But as liberated as I feel about my new life, I still feel uncertain about transition. I am still grappling just as I am considering cosmetic steps to make myself look more feminine.

I schedule a consultation in December 2013 for what is known as a tracheal shave to reduce the size of my Adam's apple, since males have bigger ones than females. My assistant Ronda Kamihira and I enact an elaborate scheme to avoid detection since such a procedure is often perceived as a precursor to transition. We decide upon a two-prong approach:

We schedule the appointment as if it is for Ronda, using a phony name. We drive to the medical building in Beverly Hills. Ronda goes in first and I trail behind to avoid any suggestion that we are there as a couple (the tabloids would eat up the story: SAYONARA, KRIS, EX-HUBBY-TO-BE HAS NEW HOTTIE). We get safely inside with no paparazzi attacks (they can be anywhere within minutes because of tips from paid snitches for the tabloids, not to mention passersby who take video with their smartphones and then try to sell it). Ronda checks in and I act as if I am just there for moral support. We go into the doctor's office together for the consultation, and it is only then in total privacy we tell him it is actually for me. We leave the same way we came, as if we are separate. Then we jump in the car and we drive home.

Roughly twenty-four hours later...

I am in my car when the phone rings. It is Harvey Levin of TMZ, the notorious gossip channel and website that, in my mind, revels in destroying others to what I imagine is the sound of its twentysomething employees laughing and tittering as they recount their gotchas on camera with Harvey sipping out of a cup taller than he is.

The call surprises me. Actually, it sickens me, since there is no one you would rather hear from less if you are in the public eye.

I pull off to the side of the road.

We heard you went in to have a consultation for a tracheal shave. I have been told that's the beginning steps of transition. It's a huge story.

How does he know all the details? The meeting with the doctor was *totally* private.

I am flustered. My back is to the wall.

I just never liked my trachea.

I have confirmed that I am thinking of having the procedure done. Which will be used by TMZ to suggest that I am in the beginning stages of transitioning into a woman.

Harvey, don't do this to me.

This is a huge story.

Harvey, please don't do this to me.

He keeps talking, but he doesn't respond to the plea.

Harvey, I haven't even spoken to all my children yet about this.

He just keeps talking.

By printing this stuff, you destroy lives.

He just keeps talking.

I can tell he couldn't care less about my pleas. He's going to print the story on their website, which will then go out all over the world with the all-but-certain implication I am becoming a woman.

I go home that night. I try to sleep but wake up in the wee hours, knowing that a story is most likely going to come out in just a few hours. I pace back and forth across the hallway. The same thought goes through me over and over.

You keep a gun in the house. Why not use it? Just get it over with.

I cannot handle this. I cannot deal with this anymore. I have already been labeled a freak in the tabloids. It will only get worse, more paparazzi than ever pursuing and trying to make a buck off of me. And my children. First and foremost my children. I am still in the process of talking to each of them individually to explain the gender issues I have had all my life. And now they are going to see some story that humiliates them and humiliates me.

I keep thinking the same thought.

You keep a gun in the house. Why not just use it?

I finally get a few hours of sleep. I leave the house the next morning and walk to an open field to get some air. I have one of my model helicopters with me. I love flying them; it's my only other outlet besides golf to get away from the chaos when I lived with Kris and the kids. I put the helicopter down and just start walking.

The breeze off the ocean helps revive me, clear my head. I realize that suicide is never the answer, although I can see how a trans person, in the heat of despair, could be driven to it. For all my pain, I have had a life that has been inspiring and positive to others. I have had every possible creature comfort. I don't want to end it. I don't want to put my kids through something like that. I think:

What a terrible way to end my story.

Why give Harvey and the tabloids the satisfaction? Because now I am curious to see how it all plays out. How does this story end?

All I want now is for the whole public mess to die down. Which it eventually does. After about a month, in January 2014, I decide to go ahead with the tracheal shave. But this time I am going to be even more careful.

I schedule the procedure at six thirty on a Sunday morning so no other patients will be there and the streets will be empty. I am driven to the office in Beverly Hills, once again by Ronda. We pull into a small alley. An assistant who works in the medical office is waiting at the back door. She lets me in, a distance of roughly two feet. The procedure takes about three hours. I am wearing a blue patient smock when I leave with a small bandage over my Adam's apple. I am a little dazed after waking up from the anesthesia. My hair is a mess, frankly witch-like. I look out of it and awful. But who cares? I just want to get home so I can sleep.

Ronda goes out the back door into the alleyway to get the car. She sees a security guard there. She returns with the car and the security guard is gone. She scans in every direction and doesn't see any paparazzi. A nurse escorts me out the back door into the car, once again a distance of two feet.

Roughly twenty-four hours later...

I am home in Malibu when I get a call from a friend.

Have you seen the Internet?

No...

There's a picture of you with a bandage on your neck. They say it means you are becoming a woman.

What?!

I go on the Internet. The story is all over the place, further fueling the rumor that I am in the process of transitioning when I myself am still not sure. Thinking seriously about it? Yes. But remember, I came close once before and pulled back.

Obviously a photographer was lurking in the shadows. But who tipped him off?

Come to think of it, where did the security guard go?

It seems that for every precaution I take there is always one more I should have taken. Like maybe never leaving the house at all. Why is everything so complicated? I am just trying to be me, find peace in my soul, and all I do is get destroyed publicly for it and laughed at.

Maybe I should leave Malibu, where I have lived for much of my forty years since the Olympics. Maybe it's better for everyone, including me, to disappear, go somewhere remote. There must be one place in the world where there aren't paparazzi and paid snitches. It is familiar soul-searching again with a slightly more emphatic result:

Fuck all these assholes.

They are not going to dictate my life. They are not going to make me leave a place I love. I am not giving in to them. Nor am I going to make it any easier for them.

They want to take a picture of me, they are going to have to work their asses off for it.

The Internet uproar over the tracheal shave has made it clear: if I am ever to come to a resolution about my life, I must finish talking to all the kids and tell them about my struggle.

I must also stop fooling around with God.

It's time for each of us to put our cards on the table.

I go to a church called the California Community Church. Kris and I founded it. The pastor there is Brad Johnson, and I trust him and feel I must talk to him privately about what I am going through and what God really thinks. Does God love me? Has he always loved me? Will he still love me? Why did he do this to me? Was it a test of my strength or a condemnation? As I have now discovered, so many trans men and women have asked themselves the very same questions.

Why *did* God do this to me? Is there a reason, and *what* is the reason?

Perhaps Pastor Brad can help me find answers.

It is a beautiful day in Malibu when I meet with him at my beachfront rental. There is a particular chair I favor in the dining area because it overlooks the Pacific Ocean and I can hear the waves crashing. Brad comes in and I sit him down in the chair so he is comfortable. I sit facing him and begin to talk.

I have some things that have been going through my head all my life, and you may be a little shocked by this. I am going to tell you a lot of things about me that you may not under-stand, but I will do my best to explain them. This is what I've dealt with all my life.

Brad just listens.

I sometimes think that when God looked down and made little Bruce, he decided to give me all these great qualities. He decided to make me handsome. He decided to make me a great athlete. He decided to make me kind. He decided to make me smart and articulate. He gave me more than any person could possibly hope for. Perfect, really. And then he threw in one little curveball to see how I would do with it, something to balance it all out and make my life a little more challenging and interest-ing. He decided to give me the soul of a female.

It was the only way I could justify in my heart that God *was not* condemning me but *was* testing my strength and resolve.

Brad then spoke. He still didn't say much. But what he did say spoke volumes.

God is not judging you. He loves you. We are all different.

I did feel great strength after I heard that. It was a turning point in going through transition without turning back.

God does love me. I have not committed a sin. Maybe this is the reason God put me on this earth, to live an authen-tic life and bring the issue of gender forward. But God is still challenging me. It is not going to be easy. But now I will have his faith to fall back on.

It's still not going to be easy.

In the process of telling all my kids, I had purposely started with Brandon because of his Gandhi-esque temperament. If anyone was going to be empathetic and supportive, I figured it would be him. I talked openly. We talked openly. He was not surprised, since his mom had told him long ago of my gender dysphoria after he wanted to know why I had breasts. I think in some sense he had been waiting for roughly twenty years.

After we talked for a while he said this to me:

Dad, I've always been proud to be your son. When I go to the airport and they ask for my ID, they always say, "Hey, is your dad Bruce Jenner? Oh, we love Bruce. He comes through here, and he's so nice." But Dad, I've never been more proud of you than I am right now.

I think that may be the nicest and most important thing anyone has ever said to me. If I could have just stopped with Brandon, I would be home free.

But nine still to go.

The older Jenner kids, in their thirties at this point, are wonderful. Like Brandon, Burt and Casey were told of my issues when they were younger and were not surprised. They, too, are euphoric for me and also proud. Brody had not been told anything until his late twenties, and was shocked and stunned. But he also felt it explained a great deal about my emotional distance and absence from his life and the lives of his siblings.

If you can't be comfortable with yourself, how can you truly be comfortable with anyone?

Then I start with the Kardashians. Kim basically already knows and is totally supportive. So is Kourtney. Khloé has the hardest time with it. She is upset because I never specifically told her I was going to transition. She is right: at that time I still did not know what I was going to do, if transition was even possible. It is something Khloé and I should talk about privately, as we have on many occasions on other sensitive subjects. But we have not, although I have tried. We have not been the same since.

Kendall and Kylie are nineteen and seventeen. Which also makes telling them the most difficult of all. I am not sure if they will understand it. Kids at that age are still tender and prone to embarrassment. They, too, are supportive. But the question posed by Kendall reverberates:

So, do we still call you Dad?

Yes. I'll be your dad always.

They have called me that ever since.

I passed an incredible hurdle in my life by telling all the kids about my issues.

I think I am about ready to transition.

There is only one problem.

How am I going to do this without being subjected to even more worldwide ridicule than I already have been? The idea of a man becoming a woman is still shocking and weird to people, ghoulishly funny. There is no place to hide.

I could move to the Sahara, and the paparazzi and the tabloids would find me.

It wouldn't become a serious story but a tabloid one:

JENNER FOUND ALIVE IN DRESS! It is too important a story, not just for me but for the trans community, to land in the gutter. It's been in the gutter since the 1980s. I am not going to let it stay there.

There is only one solution: better call Nierob.

I have not worked with Alan at Rogers and Cowan for a quarter of a century. I haven't spoken to him and am not even sure he still works there. He was a cub when he handled me in the 1980s, helping me through the storm of the *New York Times* when the rumors were rife. I knew through the grapevine that he had become one of the top public relations executives in Hollywood. He knows everyone and is highly regarded for his no-bullshit approach, not one of these people who only tell you what you want to hear.

I assume he has branched out to his own firm. But just for the hell of it I call directory assistance for Rogers and Cowan in Beverly Hills. Then I dial the number. A receptionist answers.

Can I help you?

Alan Nierob.

One second, please.

My God, he still works there.

Hello?

Alan, it's Bruce Jenner.

His first instinct is to make sure I am okay, that the mainstream media is not looking to do a story that will blow up my life.

Are you all right?

I'm fine.

That's good.

I bet you've been waiting for this call for the last thirty years.

No, not really.

It's good to know that he hasn't changed a drop.

Alan, you gotta come out this weekend. We have to sit down and talk.

We make a date. I sit him down in the exact same chair as Pastor Brad (it's my lucky chair). He already knows my story and gender issues, so I don't have to recite them again. There is one new wrinkle since we spoke about it in the 1980s.

I think I am truly ready to transition and would like to do it without being inserted into the media meat cleaver. It is also a story that needs context, as much about the transgender community and the problems it faces as about me.

How the hell can we pull this off? It cannot be something that's in the gutter because it's there right now with the tabloids. We have to find the right people who can tell this story with compassion.

Alan immediately mentions Diane Sawyer because of her reputation on sensitive stories, fair and firm but no pulling of punches and end-arounds.

He, of course, knows her and her producer Mark Robertson.

We move on to print. Alan asks me point-blank:

What would be your ideal dream choice in print?

Vanity Fair.

It is a highly credible news source. It does detailed profiles and is celebrity-driven. It's also edgy and likes to push the envelope a little bit.

Wanting Diane Sawyer and *Vanity Fair* are fine: just about everybody wants them when they think they have a story to tell. But actually getting them interested…

How are we gonna do this?

Let's see if I can deliver.

Alan issues only one caveat:

I can't effectively do this by committee. It's me and you.

Alan is aware I have ten children, none of whom shrink when it comes to opinion.

I'm in.

Mark Robertson flies out to Los Angeles the following week to meet me. Brandon is there. So is Alan. So is Ronda, whose competence and loyalty and friendship have been unlike those in any relationship I have ever had. All of them are protective of me, which makes me feel better. They are also aware of my propensity to say yes just to please someone.

Robertson is a straight shooter. Nor does he need much convincing that this is a legitimate and worthy story.

I would love to do this.

His sense is that Diane will jump at it as well. But she is on sabbatical: in the space of several weeks her husband, Mike Nichols, and her mother have died. The tragedy is incomprehensible. When Robertson goes to her apartment and approaches her in New York about the idea, she is still understandably shaken by all the losses she had to face so quickly. Robertson realizes that this simply isn't a good time. He comes back the next day and tells Diane about me and my readiness to talk openly. Diane does not hesitate. She wants to do it. She thinks it is a worthy story that will help people and make a difference. It will also be her first piece coming back to work, give her something to dive into, and help take her mind off the tragedies she has experienced.

As for *Vanity Fair*, editor Graydon Carter already broached the idea of getting my cooperation for a story, given all the rumors. Alan does not know that. He independently approaches Jane Sarkin at *Vanity Fair*. She is the features editor of the magazine and has known Alan for close to thirty years. She has handled a slew of sensitive *Vanity Fair* cover stories and photographs and also has a very close relationship with photographer Annie Leibovitz. Alan trusts Jane. Jane trusts Alan. He knows she will make sure the story is handled fairly and with sensitivity. She knows that when Alan promises something, in this case complete access to me for several months, he will not insist on a million conditions. Alan has a private conversation with Jane in early 2015. Roughly two days later he calls me.

Okay, you got the cover of Vanity *Fair.*

Holy crap, are you kidding me? I am doing this.

The magazine chooses contributing editor Buzz Bissinger to write the story. I am familiar with the book he wrote about high school football in Texas, *Friday Night Lights*. Alan vets Buzz with an old friend he grew up with in Los Angeles, Fred Mann, an editor at the *Philadelphia Inquirer* when Buzz worked there. Mann says he is firm and prickly, can be tough, but is also fair. Alan has also read some of Buzz's other work, a book he wrote about his brain-injured son called *Father's Day* and an intriguingly bizarre piece for *GQ* about his extreme leather fetish. He fits all the criteria: writing about sports, parenting, and, perhaps most important of all, what it is like to be different.

The pieces are in place. But this is an undeniably big story. Not just for the public but for me. Bigger for me. How my transition will be perceived will be contingent on how I am portrayed. Diane Sawyer will go first in an exclusive interview on ABC's *20/20* set to air on April 24, 2015. I will tell her I am transitioning (in fact I already have when the piece runs, since the actual interview was in February). This is about Bruce's struggle, what he has been dealing with all his life. So Caitlyn will not appear nor will her name be mentioned.

Roughly two months later, *Vanity Fair* will reveal my name for the first time on the cover, along with an Annie Leibovitz portrait. Alan is determined that we own the story and tell it the way we want to tell it. He doesn't want a complete circus. The way he sees it, the *20/20* interview is saying goodbye to Bruce and *Vanity Fair* is saying hello to Caitlyn.

I am very nervous when Diane comes to the beachfront

home in Malibu to interview me. The segment is scheduled for one hour. But after Diane interviews me for five hours she goes to her bosses and says the segment now needs to be two hours. I trust her totally.

Often journalists are preoccupied with questions about genitalia instead of the bigger, more pertinent issues at hand. When *Orange Is the New Black* actress Laverne Cox, who set a landmark for the transgender community with her recurring role on the show, was asked about her genitalia, she gave the perfect answer: "The preoccupation with transition and surgery objectifies trans people. And then we don't get to really deal with the real lived experiences."

Just because you are a trans woman or man, why does the media think such a question is okay? Just because you are a trans person, it doesn't mean you have to answer every question. The implication of it is obvious: you're not the real thing unless you have had gender-affirming surgery. It is beyond malarkey. You don't have to do a single thing physically to be a trans man or woman. There is no rulebook.

To trans women and men, such a question is the equivalent of asking a cisgender man how his ejaculation went today or a cisgender woman how her period is going. In other words, it's inappropriate and offensive unless a trans woman or man brings it up on their own. Sadly, it is the thing the public is preoccupied with the most, and you feel pinned into a corner and have no choice but to answer it once so there will be no more speculation. Which there will be anyway.

No matter how sensitive Diane is when she interviews me and how well versed she is on the issues facing transgender men and women, what if I say the wrong thing? What if people simply think me perverse, or inauthentic, or think I am doing it for money (I could have sold my story to the tabloids for millions if I was doing it for money), or fame beyond the role of befuddlement I have on *Keeping Up with the Kardashians*? What if I inadvertently insult the transgender community because I still know very little about it? There is no second chance here.

Because the interview is not airing live, I will be given the opportunity to reword something if upon reflection I regret saying it, standard operating procedure in interviews of this nature. Both Diane and Mark are reassuring.

This is your story, not ours.

But no matter how many times I want to reword something, I obviously will not see the segment beforehand. Plenty of reporters have promised pure intentions and then beaten the hell out of me. As much as I trust Diane and Mark, I am not naïve.

They can still crucify me.

Alan better be right.

Between the tracheal shave and my pending divorce

from Kris, the paparazzi are more relentless than ever. I live in a gated community, and any time I leave there are four or five waiting outside to take pictures and often follow. They are resourceful.

But so am I.

Because I was once a race car driver, I am pretty skilled at making stealth lefts and stealth rights and U-turns, so instead of the paparazzi following me, I am following them. There are few better feelings than watching one look into his rearview mirror and then turn around so I can wave because I am trailing behind. Sometimes they get so confused that they wait by the side of the road to reorient themselves when I drive by. That merits a nice wave as well.

On one occasion, after they chase me into the driveway of Brandon's house, I manage to block them in with my car and call the police. The most amazing part is the offended look on their faces, as if I haven't played fair.

I don't go many places, mostly to a nearby Starbucks on the Pacific Coast Highway to get my grande vanilla latte fix. I wear a baggy sweatshirt with a hood pulled over my head so they can barely see my face. I also wear the same outfit every day on the assumption that they are getting the same picture all the time and no outlet will want to buy it. The customers at Starbucks know me pretty well, and sometimes when there is a photographer lurking in the parking lot, they form a protective shield around me and escort me to my car.

They don't like that. They will regroup and redraw battle lines and retaliate: the Nail Offensive.

Several months before the *20/20* interview and the *Vanity Fair* cover, I start having girls' nights. They are informal gatherings at my house and a way of introducing the woman I will call Caitlyn to close family and friends.

There is no way I am going to host a girls' night without getting my nails done. It would be like Kim showing up at a public event in flannel pajamas. But I can't go to a manicurist. So I go to Sherwood to play golf, then sit in my car in a mostly empty parking lot afterward painting my nails, then let them dry as I drive the half hour to my home. I put one of my hands out the window so they can dry a little more quickly and I won't have to fuss with them when I get home.

I am at a stoplight. My hand is raised just enough so it is visible.

Zzzd. Zzzd. Zzzd. Zzzd.

A photographer has been following me ever since I left the golf club. He is across the street going in the opposite direction.

Zzzd. Zzzd. Zzzd. Zzzd.

It's all over the tabloids the next day and for weeks afterward.

The painted lady.

All because I raised my hand six inches too high in my car stopped at a light.

Okay, you got me on this one. Never again.

I start wearing work gloves whenever I drive.

It is impossible for my children or my mother and sisters to walk through the grocery line and not see the picture plastered on the rags. It makes me look like a fool and is extraordinarily painful to my family. And all of this is before the Diane Sawyer interview airs. What will it be like after I tell my story and publicly announce my intent to transition in front of millions?

In the weeks before the airdate, I go through my Rolodex and call people I am close to, or once was close to before I drifted away, to tell them what is happening.

I call my sister Pam. Since she has known of my issues for a long time, I doubt she will be very surprised. What does surprise me is her reaction. She tells me not to do it because she is worried I will be labeled a freak. Then she talks about what her friends will think.

I was always proud of the fact of being Bruce Jenner's sister. Eventually people find out. I watched the Olympics: what a hero he was. I was very proud of that, and now, Oh my God, how is this is going to come across?

I have to be honest: I really am not worried about what Pam's friends will think. I am worried about surviving all of this. But I now realize her reaction was really one of being scared, not just for her but also for me.

Now comes the most difficult moment of all.

Because my mom is so sharp at the age of eighty-eight and still lives on her own and still drives a Cadillac even though she can barely see over the dashboard, she knows that her son has been in the news. A few weeks earlier, she had called me to ask what was going on.

The tabloid magazines are tearing you apart and saying things that I didn't know about you wearing nail polish and that business when you went to the doctor and had a bandage. I can't help but see it every time I go to the grocery store. And if someone is writing about you, I am going to read it. I don't buy it. I go down the aisle and read it and then put it back because I don't want to contribute financially to those people. But what is going on?

I still deny everything. I just blame it on tabloid journalism, and that seems to satisfy her. My mom is a person of faith and goes regularly to church. I wonder how that part of her life will be able to deal with this.

But at the end of the conversation she says something that gives me great hope.

I don't care if it's true or false. I loved you the day you were born, and I'll never stop.

I can't put it off any longer.

I dial my mother's number.

Mom, are you sitting down?

She is sitting in a tall chair at the island in the kitchen having her coffee.

Yes, dear, I'm sitting down.

I've got something to tell you.

Okay.

You know how you've been reading all these stories about me, and actually I've been denying them and blaming it on the tabloids, but it's about time I talked to you about this. Actually there is a lot of truth to them.

A pause...

Ever since I was very little, I have suffered from gender dysphoria. I have always had this woman that has lived inside me. And it's made my life very difficult. I've had to deal with a lot of things that you didn't know throughout the years. I wasn't honest with you. I wasn't honest with anybody. But that Diane Sawyer interview is going to come up and you're going to hear a lot of things that you probably didn't know about me. But it's going to be okay.

A pause.

Now it is my mom's turn to say something.

Why didn't I know? What could I have done? You were in pain. This is my fault.

Mom, it had nothing to do with you. This is just kind of the way I am made.

Well, I could have done better. Why didn't I see this?

We talk several more times in the days that follow. She still feels guilt in not having detected anything as I was growing up and helping to alleviate it. But typical of my mom, she begins to copiously read about the issue of gender dysphoria on the Internet. The more we talk about the issues, the better she feels and the better I feel. She is relieved to finally get an answer to why I held myself at arm's length when I was growing up, how there had always been a subtle discomfort. She realizes that none of this had *anything* to do with the way I was brought up.

With each conversation our relationship, never a perfect line, draws closer and closer.

Of course, she's my mom. So she still worries.

She braces herself for what will happen when I go public on television.

She is not the only one.

—ɷ—

Chapter Thirteen

The Looking Glass

I watch the segment at the home in Hidden Hills where Kris and I once lived together. It is ABC's East Coast feed, so it begins at six p.m. All the Kardashian kids are there with the exception of Robert. Kendall and Kylie are on opposite sides of me on a couch in the living room. Kris is behind us in a chair by herself. How shocked or not she is by my transition is immaterial at this moment: it has to be very, very, weird to see your former husband of twenty-three years and with whom you have two children go on television in front of an estimated 17.1 million people and say:

...For all intents and purposes, I am a woman.

Wow...

I can't believe I just said that.

I am a woman.

Do you know how incredible that sounds from my lips, how I never ever thought those words would come except in moments of privacy with a handful of others, how I was convinced I would die with a life that was incomplete?

I am a woman.

The secret is out after sixty-five years.

I am a woman.

Say it again to the heavens so God can hear it and smile.

I AM A WOMAN!!!!

Jesus, Jenner, what took you so long?

Kendall and Kylie, who between them have close to 200 million followers on Instagram and Twitter (the couch collectively has close to 500 million), start hitting the social media channels almost immediately after the interview has begun. Their sisters join in.

Here it comes....

Kendall gives the initial results.

Dad, you should see the reaction you are already getting! It's incredible.

It is a great moment.

But frankly I am worried about logistics.

I go over to Casey's house in Santa Monica and make it in time to watch the West Coast feed at nine p.m. All the Jenner kids are there and their spouses and significant others as well as Chrystie and Linda. They, too, are elated with how the segment went. Everybody in the three families is happy.

At least for a day.

Several of the Jenner children were interviewed during

the show, as were my mother and sister. The Kardashian side feels slighted by their noticeable absence. They are right to feel slighted. They were slighted on purpose because of research showing that anytime a Kardashian is on television, many in the public tend to think it is a publicity stunt to make money. I love my kids, and the last thing on Earth I ever want to do is somehow think I am rejecting them. But because of the research, I needed to build a wall and distance myself for this interview. It was too important. After all of the time it took to get here, I needed to make clear that this is real, this is my life and not some publicity stunt. I couldn't afford to add any fuel to the rumor that I was only doing it for money. I only had one chance. This had to be about me and only me. If I screwed up, at least it would be on my own terms.

Much to my relief, the public reaction is phenomenal. My honesty and sincerity have come through, no doubt because I have one great advantage—I only know how to be candid, regardless of repercussion. The level of interest was amazing as well: the show had the highest ratings for the newsmagazine in more than fifteen years, and the highest rated non–sports network show on a Friday night in twelve years.

I have made it through whole. I am still in one piece.

But I'm not quite done yet.

Wait until they see Caitlyn for the first time.

Everybody has advice about what I should wear for

the *Vanity Fair* photo shoot. The older Jenner children really want me to tone it down, elegant but not too flashy or revealing. Their intentions are good: they want me to set the right tone of womanhood as they define it. They are also sincerely worried that the more glam I try to be, the more I will feed the accusations of exploitation. They are trying to protect me. But their vision of womanhood is not my vision of womanhood: the most resonant advice comes from Kim, who, as she points out, doesn't simply know fashion but *is* fashion.

You gotta rock it.

Before the actual *Vanity Fair* shoot we need to go back in time a little bit. Because there is an actual date, a literal moment when Bruce takes a final bow and Caitlyn steps onto the stage.

March 15, 2015.

Several days earlier I had played golf by myself one final time at Sherwood, hitting three balls on each hole before I quit after the seventh and eat a steak sandwich in the dim womb of the clubhouse. I sit lonely in my house one final time watching television. I am in my cocoon of isolation one final time. Or am I? Will the comfort I hope to feel as a woman only lead to discomfort in others? Will people look at me and say privately to themselves, "My God, what have you done to yourself?" Will I think the same thing?

What have I done to myself?

I do not feel scared. I feel confident that this is the right thing to do. I am excited. But when you have surgery such as this, there is no turning back. There is no oops, I made a mistake, just put everything back the way it was.

The questions are daunting. The answers even more so.

I leave the house in Malibu at four fifteen a.m. Ronda is once again driving. The appointment is not until six a.m. at a surgical center in Beverly Hills, but I hate being late for anything. Plus I doubt that the paparazzi are up at this early hour hoping to snap my picture. We take the Pacific Coast Highway to I-10 east to I-405 north and then into Beverly Hills. Ronda, who knows my moods better than anyone, can tell that I am nervous. Sometimes small talk can often lessen those feelings, but not now. I just want to get this over with. I am tired thinking about it.

Pioneered in the 1980s and 1990s by San Francisco plastic surgeon Douglas Ousterhout, facial feminization surgery involves hairline correction, forehead contouring, and jaw and chin contouring. I will also have a procedure to augment my breasts.

For me, and speaking *only* for me, the feeling is that if I'm going to do it, then I might as well do it. Every trans woman or man has her or his definition of authenticity. I want to look as physically a woman as I possibly can, based on my own image. I will never feel like a woman if I don't have the surgery. I also have the luxury of being able to afford such an extensive procedure.

It is not something I suddenly thought I should have. One way or another I have thought about altering my appearance for almost fifty years.

I have chosen the facial plastic surgeon Harrison Lee, who has offices in Beverly Hills and New York and is one of the best surgeons of this type in the country. The actual procedure will be in the Beverly Hills offices of Gary Alter, who has equally impeccable credentials and will do the breast augmentation.

The Los Angeles Marathon is being held on the same day. So we carefully map out the route to avoid street closures. We arrive at five a.m., before the sun is even up, another component of the cat-and-mouse game that is my life: always try to get there when it's still dark out. By prearrangement we drive into an alley behind the clinic where the surgery will take place. A nurse is there to meet us, and it's only a matter of three or four steps before I am in the office. I now have three security officers scanning every nook and cranny.

Lee has thoroughly gone over all the steps of the procedure well beforehand. I think it will take maybe five hours. It takes around ten, not that I remember anything since I am out cold from anesthesia. I hate surgeries. I hate going under the knife. I hate getting knocked out. I hate waking up groggy and disoriented and dizzy.

I am under for about twelve hours before I wake up at roughly seven p.m. Security personnel are now roaming the halls of the office looking for paparazzi. They help me through the back door into a waiting black van. My head is spinning during the entirety of the hour-and-a-half ride back to Malibu. I am lying down in a corner of the van, dozing in and out, and it seems like it is taking forever when all I want to do is get home. My face is fully bandaged, so I can barely see. My breasts are bandaged as well. In normal circumstances I would spend the night in the hospital in case of complications. But these are not normal circumstances, and the risk of discovery too great, since hospitals are notorious celebrity cesspools for leaks. So Dr. Lee comes home with me and so does a nurse. They spend the night along with Ronda.

It becomes perhaps the most difficult night of my life.

I want to fully wake up but I can't because I was out for so long. I keep trying to get my senses about me.

Wake up!

That's all I keep thinking.

Wake up!

But when I close my eyes my head is still spinning and I can feel the drugs coursing through my body and this is now several hours after the surgery. I shut my eyes and I finally think I am getting some sleep. Then I open them and look at the clock next to my bed and only two minutes have gone by.

I try again.

Two minutes.

Again.

Two minutes.

Again.

This time it's not even close to two minutes. My eyes shoot open. My heartbeat becomes so loud I can hear it. *Ka-thump. Ka-thump. Ka-thump.* My adrenal glands are pumping.

This has never happened to me before. I am always in control of my emotions, but not tonight. *Get a grip. Just get a grip. Try to take a deep breath. In. Out. Another. In. Out.*

It's not working.

I am having a panic attack.

Every question that I had before the surgery hits me again, only this time like a stream of bullets. Without embellishing—and I swear I am not embellishing—it is like I am convulsing inside.

What the fuck did you just do?

What the fuck did you just do?!

Stop it. Just stop it!

I can't.

What the fuck did you just do?!!

Louder inside my head.

WHAT THE FUCK DID YOU JUST DO??!!

The cold dread of fear.

The public may be accepting of me in the *20/20* piece. But I was still Bruce when the cameras rolled. They haven't seen me with my face altered and augmented breasts.

I haven't seen me!

What if I look in the mirror for the first time and see a complete stranger?

Who is this person?

What if I look in the mirror and hate the way I look just like I did before? What if I regret this?

Oh, God…

Please, God.

Don't desert me now.

Don't do it.

The nurse is right beside me in the room. I put my feet down on the floor.

Turn on the TV!

I need distractions, noise, anything. I can't go where my head is going right now.

Just the noise. Please just the noise. That will help. I know it will help.

It doesn't.

I walk out of the bedroom and start pacing in the adjacent hallway.

That will help get this out of me. I know it will.

It doesn't.

The questions are flying fast and furious now.

One after another after another with no space in between.

How am I going to be accepted? How are my kids going to accept me? Are you going to be considered a freak from this point on? Here you were the big, big jock Bruce Jenner, and now all of a sudden you're not. You're not. Not even close to that. What is my mother going to think? What is my sister going to think? What am I going to think?

I will pace all night if I have to. I'm not shutting my eyes again.

The questions die down a little bit. The panic turns into something a little bit softer and easier to manage. It isn't questions that fill my head now but another thought entirely.

It can't be worse than the other side where I came from.

The thought builds and now there is a slice of comfort.

I can make this work. I will make it work!

I am going to live authentically for the first time in my life. I am going to learn every single issue facing the brothers and sisters of the transgender community. I am going to raise money. I am going to start a foundation. I am going to use my public platform to tirelessly speak on the issues. I am going to have an enthusiasm for life that I have not had in thirty-nine years since the Olympics, almost two-thirds of my life.

I will make a difference because I am different.

The pacing back and forth helps. The panic attack subsides.

It never comes back again.

The only problem now is that I look like hell, as if my face was thrown in the dryer on high heat and then ironed. It is not a pretty sight, and the fear is that I am going to end up looking like Michael Jackson. But after roughly six weeks the swelling has gone down and almost all the scars have disappeared.

I look like...Well, who do I look like?

You try picking out a permanent new name for yourself after sixty-five years.

It's weird.

I had thought of names as far back as Graceland. There

was a singing group at college called the Serendipity Singers and one of their numbers was a song called "Heather." I thought Heather might be a cool name because the song was so cool. But after college the name faded away. I thought about something simple, like Mary. Then when Kris and I got together I felt obligated to pick a name that began with *K*, which is when Kathy popped into my head. But Kathy seemed like…well…Kathy.

So one of my favorite pastimes became watching the Miss Universe and Miss America pageants with pen and paper in hand to jot down the names of all the different contestants. I was hoping there was one I particularly liked whose name I would also like. But I struck out and never did settle on one that seemed just right.

Until I became a woman.

Now I really did need to find a name for the rest of my life.

I went back to Heather, but I really wasn't crazy about it. I talked to Ronda about the naming dilemma, how whenever I thought I had found one that works, I ended up getting bored with it after a while. Ronda made her own suggestion:

I've always liked the name Caitlyn.

I had thought about Caitlyn back in the K period, which meant it would have been spelled Kaitlyn. Or Kaitlin. However it was spelled, there was no way I was going to have a name now that began with a *K*. That would have been beyond creepy.

Which is when Ronda chimed in again:

I always liked the spelling of C-A-I-T-L-Y-N.

So Caitlyn it will be. I choose the middle name Marie simply because I like it. I leave the last name Jenner intact, even though at a certain point I had thought of changing it to get away from my past life as much as possible (I am glad I didn't).

Caitlyn.

Caitlyn Marie.

Caitlyn Marie Jenner.

I can get used to that.

But I am not sure everyone is totally happy with it.

I was with Kim one day when she asked me:

Well, what are we going to call you?

It's Caitlyn.

You stuck with the Ks, huh?

I'm spelling it with a C.

Oh. I'm kind of disappointed.

Spoken like a true Kardashian.

So now that I have a name, what's left?

The final hurdle, when all I do is tell the world who I now am and show them what I now look like.

Several weeks before the shoot Annie Leibovitz comes out to the house to scout the site and get to know me a little better. *Vanity Fair*'s fashion and style director Jessica Diehl flies out from New York to meet with me as well and find out what I like and what I don't—or more accurately, what I shouldn't wear, tactfully steering me away from the big fashion statement in favor of a mix of what she describes as Rene Russo in *The Thomas Crown Affair* meets Angelina Jolie, elegant with a dash of tough.

The day before the shoot, she and her assistant Ryan Young return for a fitting.

I had always fantasized about having beautiful clothes that fit. As many times as I had stood in front of hotel mirrors and thought I looked good, I always knew it could be better. Just as I also had convinced myself I would never get the opportunity.

So now...

Some apparel has been shipped previously, other items were brought by Diehl and Young on the flight to Los Angeles. There are well over a hundred different pieces— gowns, blouses, sweaters, belts, cocktail dresses, lingerie, jewelry, heels, high heels. So many items that a temporary tent is built on my sizeable deck. What is perhaps most amazing of all is that none of the haute couture shops where Diehl and Young searched for clothing in New York asked who exactly these items were for, given the person was six-foot-two. Diehl thinks it's because I have the look of a 1980s Amazonian model with a slender frame, which is what I may want carved on my tombstone, along with a quote from Diehl saying I look perfect in Tom Ford.

I have trouble initially believing that this is all for me to try on, the only goal being to make me look my best.

Ninety percent of the clothing fits. It is the first time I have ever openly tried on women's clothing in front a group of strangers. It is so easy, so natural, so effortless, so fun, the way my life was always supposed to be.

Annie comes to the house the next day to take the pictures for the magazine cover, arriving with a caravan of assistants to rival that of Genghis Khan. Several editors from the magazine are here, including Jane Sarkin. So is Dana Brown, the editor on the 11,000-word piece by Buzz that will be published in several weeks in the July issue that actually comes out in early June (I have no idea why magazines do it this way). Jessica Diehl is obviously still here to make sure that the outfits Annie ultimately choses for the shoot will fit perfectly. There are also two professional stylists for hair and makeup.

Are you kidding me?

Security is airtight so news of the photo shoot will not leak. Those attending must leave their cars in the parking lot at Zuma Beach in Malibu. They are picked up by a nondescript white van driven by a member of the security detail and then transported up a winding road to the driveway of my house. Once there they are required to turn in their cellphones, after which they will be escorted inside. I have already had a temporary wall built around my house to block out the paparazzi, who over the past several weeks have taken photos from roughly a mile across the canyon using supertelephoto lenses.

The shoot lasts for two days. Annie Leibovitz is Annie

Leibovitz, after all. She has a clear vision of how she wants me to look—a little bit forties Hepburn, a little bit Vargas girl, glamorous and beautiful and a touch of sexy. The photo of me that is chosen for the cover, posing in a cream-colored bustier with perfect makeup and hair and a headline that simply says CALL ME CAITLYN, will become instantly iconic. It is the photograph that everyone will remember me by.

But the pose I remember the most takes place in the garage of my house, which has been converted into a studio. All the junk that has accumulated over the years, including the accordion, has temporarily disappeared. I am wearing an off-the-shoulder black gown by Zac Posen. It is killer, if I do say so myself. All the lights in the garage have been turned off, leaving only the ones set up for the shoot. There is dark everywhere else except on me, a kind of spotlight effect. There is a large mirror; Annie tells one of her assistants to move it behind the camera so I can actually see myself.

Not every day of my life will be spent with hair and makeup and beautiful clothing handpicked by a stylist with Annie Leibovitz taking my photograph. It is safe to say that no day of my life will ever be spent this way again.

But in that moment, when I look into the mirror, I truly see myself for the first time. So many other times I had looked into the mirror with familiar loathing and disgust.

But now...

Now the view from the looking glass is different.
I see who I am.
I am who I know.
I know who I am.
I am Caitlyn.
Caitlyn Marie Jenner.
Forever forward.

—◈—

September 17, 2016

"I am ready to seize the day."

We are waiting for the moon to rise over Malibu.

It is a perfect night atop the ridge of Decker Canyon, no fog rolling in from the Pacific Ocean, no cloud formations spreading darkness through the Santa Monica Mountains. The temperature is in the seventies, and the usual wind has simmered down to a refreshing breeze.

It is good to be home.

I am hosting an after–Labor Day cocktail party on the back patio, something I did not do a lot of back in the Bruce era. Actually, I don't think I ever did it at all.

Some of the guests are old friends who supported me in my most difficult days in the late 1980s. Some are new friends I have made, trans women who have become soul sisters, members of the gay and lesbian community and straights. Together they form a rainbow from the worst period to my happiest one.

Perhaps the best proof of how far I have come: I like being around people now. I want to be around people now.

I like parties, when for sixty-five years of my life I hated them because I felt socially awkward and insecure. I like them now because I am comfortable with myself.

Comfortable.

Not a particularly complex word. Yet a feeling so difficult for too many of us to attain because of all the roadblocks.

I am Caitlyn. I am a woman. What does that mean to be a woman now that I have been one for eighteen months?

How should I know?

You can't learn how to be a woman. A woman has been inside me all my life, and I just have to let her live. There is no guide or checklist except those meaningless stereotypes. Each of us is distinct and different, so self-evident yet so difficult for so many people to accept or embrace. We all have choices. We all make choices. We should be allowed to make them without threat.

It is why I have written this book, so that you see through my life the pain and compromises and inevitable unhappiness that accompany you wherever you go when you cannot make those choices even though they are embedded in your soul. I have written this book to help us see that there is no right way to be, or wrong way to be, or any way to be except who you are. I have written this book to show all the obstacles to equal rights that exist in the community that I love and am so proudly a part of, the transgender community. I have written this book because I am lucky to have a public platform and want to use it. I have written this book because there is a way out no matter how long it takes.

There is no magic wand. There is no sprinkling of fairy dust and *poof!*, you're completely different. When I became Caitlyn in March 2015, I didn't wake up and immediately have an urge to cook and clean or sew or do any of the other tasks that women are still assumed to do in a society still dominated by men. Nor, for that matter, did I run to the bookstore and buy books by such land-mark feminists as Betty Friedan and Gloria Steinem. All I can say is that I am evolving. Gender is a journey whoever you are: thoughts change, circumstances change, your view of what is important changes, the world changes.

It is easier for me to show emotions now, although it will never be easy. I feel so much more connected to the world now. I get up in the morning and get out of bed and look in the mirror and everything is in kind of the right spot—well, almost everything. I put on the clothes I want to put on without the perpetual fear that someone will see me or discover me. I go out and do the things I want to do without assuming a mask. My life is so much simpler now, no more a thousand steps for a sliver of authenticity.

I am ready to seize the day, learn something, get some-thing done, after so many years in which I just wanted the day to end. I can talk to women now instead of being envious of them or removed from them because of fear of discovery or just feeling like I never fit in, because up until I transitioned I never did.

Hell, I don't even golf alone anymore. One of the best times of the week is Tuesday, when I play at Sherwood in a women's foursome, where we gab and laugh and trade style tips and I outdrive them by 150 yards and they still like me. In a men's foursome I would hear the grumblings of competitive jealousy all the way into the next county.

There is the inevitable and cosmic question of what it all means now besides the option of hitting off the women's tee if I feel like it. It is a little presumptuous to answer—I still have enough trouble figuring out what to wear in the morning—but I also feel I should try given my lengthy journey.

Appreciation. Beauty. Freedom. Joy. Liberation. Love. Simplicity. And of course comfort. There are many more descriptive words. I don't want to double the length of the book. But maybe it all boils down to this:

Please, I am begging you, don't ever let your life succumb to what others think. Do not give into fear, as I did for so many years. Do what is in your heart and soul. I guarantee you will never ever regret it. Instead, you will have the very opposite, not an imagined life but a life of new possibility, a true life. The more we celebrate our difference, the more we will be celebrated. There are too many of us out there anyway just waiting to bloom and blossom. The status quo of society will just have to get used to us.

Not everything is perfect. It is foolish to think that everything will be.

I am still trying to sort out my relationship with all my children. I thought transition would draw us closer.

Initially it did. But over the past several months there has been a void, a distance, with many of them.

Sometimes as parents we aren't always aware of how unavailable we are in the best circumstances. Then as we grow older we have that feeling of wanting to be with our children when they can't because of their own full and busy lives. It is a circle of life where they can't always be there. It seems like they are doing the same thing we wish we hadn't done, but it's part of human nature and our own foibles. I want them to be more attentive, but how attentive was I when some of them were growing up?

But I worry that my transitioning has been harder for them to cope with than they have let on, because in public their support for me has been stirring. But perhaps there is private embarrassment. Perhaps it is weird to call me "Dad" when I don't look like Dad. I know that Burt and Brandon and Brody did not like the *Vanity Fair* cover, not only because they thought it was too risqué, but because I did not gauge how a son would feel seeing his father in a cream-colored bustier.

Fair enough.

Perhaps there are aspects of Caitlyn they hoped would be different. Although I feel much more empathy on the inside, I still have trouble showing it on the outside. Although I am observant of others, I still talk about myself too much. Maybe some of the kids feel I spend too much time over the way I look, an admittedly radical departure from Bruce, who never worried about the way he looked. I am aware that in the newness of being a trans woman there is a tendency to have an initial period of pseudo-adolescence, in which makeup and clothing become your touchstones of discovery, a way of feeling liberated. So maybe that will change.

I wonder if I should sit down with the kids individually just as I did before transition so each can talk candidly with me and I can talk candidly with them. Just as gender is a journey, so is the relationship you have with your children after you transition. Nothing comes instantly or overnight. There is no perfect.

I know what it is like to be lonely. I was lonely for most of my life. My greatest fear now is that I will one day revert to that same kind of loneliness, a prisoner of my house when the big difference now is that I don't want to be a prisoner. I am scared of becoming a hermit again, probably because past so often is prologue, at a time in my life when Caitlyn sees the possibilities of the world that Bruce never saw.

I still spend many nights alone. I still fear that I will be a loner even though I no longer want to be one. Maybe it is just ingrained into my soul like my womanhood. Just as core beliefs don't change, maybe certain traits of personality don't either. But I am going to give it a hell of a try to break the habit. Caitlyn is too much damn fun. Bruce fundamentally disappeared the last ten years of his life. Plus, talking about the Olympics does get old, very old. Two days of my life lasted for more than thirty years. There is so much more.

All the attention I have gotten over the past eighteen months has been fun and wonderful. But attention inevitably fades. That's okay. It is family that sustains you, not attention from people you don't even know. As I do get older I become more vulnerable. I face my mortality, and I don't want to face it alone.

My mom worries about me becoming lonely again. She thinks it would be nice for me to find a companion.

So there you have it.

If the problems facing the LGBTQ community in the United States are formidable, they are a hundred times more severe in Africa. Homosexuality is outlawed in thirty-eight African nations. Any trans woman or man who appears in public and is identified as such faces the real risk of being severely beaten or killed. At minimum, arrest by authorities is a virtual given. I would like to go to Africa, although I know that my presence in many places would not be welcome. But it would draw attention, always the first step in overturning horrible conditions.

But I will never stop fighting on behalf of the trans community here. I love America. I am proud of America. Whatever political views I have, they will never interfere with doing everything I can to help a community that has been so unfairly maligned and marginalized. I will talk with anyone at any time about the issues of job discrimination and teen suicide and violence. If I can move the needle an inch, then I have moved something.

Then there is the issue of the Final Surgery. It is a

complex decision under any circumstance, only made more complex because of the inherent risk of any operation at my age. I know it has been done thousands of times at this point and is pretty much perfected. But it is still surgery, and there are steps that have to be taken beforehand, including several sessions of electrolysis to remove hair and also an orchiectomy to remove the testicles.

It is also a matter of total personal choice. Only about 30 percent of trans women have any type of surgery, either because of the expense or because they don't feel it is necessary for their own authenticity.

So why even consider it?

Because it's just a penis. It has no special gifts or use for me other than what I have said before, the ability to take a whiz in the woods. I just want to have all the right parts. I am also tired of tucking the damn thing in all the time.

But I hate the thought of going under general anesthesia. I am also not a young person anymore. So over the past eighteen months I have gone back and forth. I lean toward having it done, and then I hesitate.

There is something about the moon tonight that is taking me in a thousand directions. Maybe because it's the residual of the harvest moon that took place the night before, a glow and orb all its own.

I think of my dad and what he would have thought of it all. I think of my mom, now ninety years old, whose acceptance of me and determination to learn about the issues puts to shame every parent who refuses to understand the pain of a child growing up in the wrong gender. I think of my brother, Burt, hovering above us, not quite believing that he now has another big sister in the family and no doubt chuckling to himself. I think of friends I have not thanked enough. I think of my children and how I can only give them the one thing any of us can truly give, which is love. I think of successes. I think of failures. I think of Bruce. It is only in becoming Caitlyn that I have realized he was a good man.

The moon rises slowly and pivots over the mountains. Its glow is hypnotic.

We all look in the silence of wonder.

Because there still is wonder in the world for all of us.

You never know what will happen.

You just never do.

Wait...

I knew I forgot something.

After much deliberation, I had The Final Surgery in January 2017. The surgery was a success, and I feel not only wonderful but liberated. I am telling you because I believe in candor. So all of you can stop staring. You want to know, so now you know. Which is why this is the first time, and the last time, I will ever speak of it.

—〰—

Acknowledgments

The trouble with thanking people is you can't do it all in the same sentence, so everyone gets the exact same amount of credit. The book could not have been done without the commitment and belief of so many.

You have to start somewhere, in my case with Alan Nierob. Alan is not only a consummate public relations executive. He not only watches my back and has my best interests at heart. He has been a friend for nearly thirty years, standing with me through difficult times and beautiful ones.

CAA literary agent Cait Hoyt was exceptional, handling every panicked phone call with grace and aplomb. Rounding out my wonderful team was my agent at CAA Jeff Frasco and my attorney Jeff Bernstein.

There would be no book without a publisher. I found a fantastic one in Grand Central Publishing. Executive editor Gretchen Young was smart, kind, and patiently persistent in making sure this book was everything it should be. She made her suggestions quietly, then kept on making them until they were adopted. Copyeditor Lori Paximadis caught about a billion things large and small.

Others at the publishing house who made significant contributions include publisher Jamie Raab, editor-in-chief Deb Futter, publicity director Jimmy Franco, managing editor Melanie Gold, marketing director Brian McLendon, art director Anne Twomey, and the divine editorial assistant Katherine Stopa.

Transcriptionist Annie Snyder, who may know more about me than anyone alive given the thousands of pages she typed, is the best in the business from the faraway land of Oregon. Valuable research was supplied by Maria Spano. Caleb Bissinger superbly did the arduous and crucial process of fact-checking. I am not sure where my assistant Ronda Kamihira fits into this puzzle, except that she did anything and everything that was asked of her as always.

I would like to thank Wendy Roth not only for her friendship over these many years but supplying us with several of the photographs that appear in this book.

I probably see more of my hairstylist Courtney and makeup stylist Kip than anyone in the world these days. They not only do expert work, they keep me sane with their chatter and laughter.

Thanks must go to Dr. Christine Milrod, instrumental in helping me through the wrenching process of talking to my children about my gender dysphoria. My pastor Brad Johnson helped me deal with the issue of my faith during the transition process.

In navigating the thicket of issues that affect the transgender community, you will not find a group of individuals who know them better and have been so willing to share their knowledge with me: Nick Adams; Kate Bornstein; Jenny Boylan; Zackary Drucker, and Margaret Hoover.

I want to thank *I Am Cait* soul sisters Candis Cayne, Ella Giselle, and Chandi Moore for taking me under their wing after I transitioned and helping me navigate a world that was so different to me. I also want to thank them for yelling at me only when they found out just how conservative I am.

I must give a huge shout-out to my children for putting up with me for all these years and offering incredible support as I went through the process of transition: in alphabetical order (there are many egos involved here): Brandon, Brody, Burt, Casey, Kendall, Khloe, Kim, Kourtney, Kylie, and Robert. Together you have shaped and saved my life many times over.

To my three ex-wives, Chrystie, Linda, and Kris: I shared a large portion of my life with each of you and while the marriages faded my continued love and respect have not. We also share in common the greatest children in the world.

My sister Pam Mettler is remarkable in so many ways. I idolized her as a child and the same is true now. She was one of the first I ever confided in because I knew I could trust her with my secret. My other sister, Lisa, has also been there for me.

Then there is my mom, Esther. It is safe to say that none of this would have happened without her, since she is the one responsible for my physical presence. I was so scared to tell her, not only because she is my mom, but eighty-eight years old at the time. The news of Caitlyn's emergence wasn't easy for her, but she has handled it with understanding, enthusiasm, and an abundance of love. And yes, Mom, I know I need to visit more.

Last but most definitely not least, I would like to thank Buzz Bissinger. His assistance on this project was invaluable. We spent over a thousand hours together; his dedication was relentless in pushing me deeper and deeper into my soul. I have a tendency to meander all over the place when I talk, and Buzz was somehow able to take all my different memories and thoughts and help fashion them into coherence.

I first met Buzz in March 2015 when he was assigned to write the story of my life and transition for *Vanity Fair.* I feel like we have been together every day since, given the intense rigors of doing a book like this. Every time I turned around he was there—a little scary if you have ever seen the way he dresses. He can be a little moody (actually very moody). He can be a little snappish (actually very snappish). But if you can get past the black leather and the skull rings and the black-polished fingernails, he is warm and funny. He is a wonderful writer, but just as important to me, he has become a wonderful friend. I also know that this book never ever would have taken shape without him.

About the Authors

Caitlyn Jenner broke the world record in the decathlon by scoring 8,634 points at the 1976 Olympic Games in Montreal. She subsequently became a broadcaster for ABC and NBC, regularly appeared on *Good Morning America*, and became one of the country's most-sought-after inspirational speakers in detailing her remarkable Olympic success.

Since revealing her true self, Caitlyn executive-produced *I Am Cait*, the award-winning series on E! hailed for raising public awareness of transgender issues. She was named Barbara Walters's Most Fascinating Person of the Year in 2015, honored as one of *Glamour* magazine's Women of the Year, and received the Arthur Ashe Award for Courage at the 2015 ESPY Awards for her transition from Olympic athlete to transgender activist.

Buzz Bissinger is a Pulitzer Prize winner and the author of the iconic *Friday Night Lights*. His other nonfiction books include *A Prayer for the City*, *Three Nights in August*, and *Father's Day*. He has been a longtime contributing editor to *Vanity Fair* and wrote the magazine's landmark cover story on Caitlyn for the July 2015 issue. He is also a professor of nonfiction writing at the University of Pennsylvania.